World History

The United States and Russia

A Cold and Complex History

By Gary Wiener

LUCENT PRESS

Published in 2018 by
Lucent Press, an Imprint of Greenhaven Publishing, LLC
353 3rd Avenue
Suite 255
New York, NY 10010

Designer: Seth Hughes
Editor: Nicole Horning

Library of Congress Cataloging-in-Publication Data

Names: Wiener, Gary, author.
Title: The United States and Russia : a cold and complex history / Gary Wiener.
Description: New York : Lucent Press, 2018. | Series: World history |
Includes bibliographical references and index.
Identifiers: LCCN 2017039398 | ISBN 9781534562455 (library bound book) | ISBN 9781534563117 (paperback book)
Subjects: LCSH: United States–Foreign relations–Russia (Federation)–Juvenile literature. | Russia (Federation)–Foreign relations–United States–Juvenile literature.
Classification: LCC E183.8.R9 W58 2018 | DDC 327.73047086–dc23
LC record available at https://lccn.loc.gov/2017039398

Printed in the United States of America

CPSIA compliance information: Batch #CW18KL: For further information contact Greenhaven Publishing LLC, New York, New York at 1-844-317-7404.

Please visit our website, www.greenhavenpublishing.com. For a free color catalog of all our high-quality books, call toll free 1-844-317-7404 or fax 1-844-317-7405.

Contents

Foreword

History books are often filled with names and dates—words and numbers for students to memorize for a test and forget once they move on to another class. However, what history books should be filled with are great stories, because the history of our world is filled with great stories. Love, death, violence, heroism, and betrayal are not just themes found in novels and movie scripts. They are often the driving forces behind major historical events.

When told in a compelling way, fact is often far more interesting—and sometimes far more unbelievable—than fiction. World history is filled with more drama than the best television shows, and all of it really happened. As readers discover the incredible truth behind the triumphs and tragedies that have impacted the world since ancient times, they also come to understand that everything is connected. Historical events do not exist in a vacuum. The stories that shaped world history continue to shape the present and will undoubtedly shape the future.

The titles in this series aim to provide readers with a comprehensive understanding of pivotal events in world history. They are written with a focus on providing readers with multiple perspectives to help them develop an appreciation for the complexity of the study of history. There is no set lens through which history must be viewed, and these titles encourage readers to analyze different viewpoints to understand why a historical figure acted the way they did or why a contemporary scholar wrote what they did about a historical event. In this way, readers are able to sharpen their critical-thinking skills and apply those skills in their history classes. Readers are aided in this pursuit by formally documented quotations and annotated bibliographies, which encourage further research and debate.

Many of these quotations come from carefully selected primary sources, including diaries, public records, and contemporary research and writings. These valuable primary sources helps readers hear the voices of those who directly experienced historical events, as well as the voices of biographers and historians who provide a unique perspective on familiar topics. Their voices all help history come alive in a vibrant way.

As students read the titles in this series, they are provided with clear context in the form of maps, timelines, and informative text. These elements give them the basic facts they need to fully appreciate the high drama that is history.

The study of history is difficult at times—not because of all the information that needs to be memorized, but because of the challenging questions it asks us. How could something as horrible as the Holocaust happen? Why would religious leaders use torture during the Inquisition? Why does ISIS have so many followers? The information presented in each title gives readers the tools they need to confront these questions and participate in the debates they inspire.

As we pore over the stories of events and eras that changed the world, we come to understand a simple truth: No one can escape being a part of history. We are not bystanders; we are active participants in the stories that are being created now and will be written about in history books decades and even centuries from now. The titles in this series help readers gain a deeper appreciation for history and a stronger understanding of the connection between the stories of the past and the stories they are part of right now.

SETTING THE SCENE: A TIMELINE

1809

The Russian Empire grants formal recognition to the United States.

1867

The Russian Empire sells Alaska to the United States.

1917

The Russian Revolution takes place in March and November.

1933

Under President Franklin Delano Roosevelt, the United States grants formal recognition to the Soviet Union.

1941

Hitler invades the Soviet Union, and the United States enters World War II as a Soviet ally.

1962

The Cuban Missile Crisis puts the United States and Soviet Union on the brink of World War III.

1973 · 1989 · 1991 · 2000 · 2016

1991 The Soviet Union dissolves.

1989 The Berlin Wall comes down.

2016 The Russian Federation interferes in the U.S. presidential election.

1973 U.S. troops pull out of Vietnam.

2000 Vladimir Putin becomes President of the Russian Federation.

INTRODUCTION

ICONIC MOMENTS IN RUSSIAN-AMERICAN RELATIONS

The United States and Russia have a complicated relationship, and there are a few famous remarks around which one can begin to understand how these two world powers came to view one another. These remarks were all spoken during the "Cold War," the period from 1947 to 1991 when tensions between the two countries were at their peak and when the Soviet Union and the United States inched closer to World War III. It was inevitable that the United States and the Soviet Union, the two remaining superpowers after World War II, would each seek to establish a dominant position in world affairs. Their leaders quarreled, then sought an easing of tensions now known as a "détente." In the process, they uttered some of the most famous words of the 20th century. Such iconic statements are so well-known that they have become part of pop culture, and almost every American who lived through that era recognizes them immediately.

A War of Words

In 1956, former Soviet Premier Nikita Khrushchev escalated tensions between his country and the West when he told a group of foreign ambassadors that he would bury them. Historians still debate whether he meant this warning literally or not, and Khrushchev later took back his words. However, many Americans interpreted his death threat as a direct reference to the Soviet Union's growing nuclear armaments. Khrushchev did equal harm to Soviet-American relations in another iconic moment, four years later, when he is said to have angrily banged his shoe on the table at the United Nations after listening to a harsh critique of Soviet dominance in Europe. Many Americans came to feel that the Soviet Union was being run by a madman, who also happened to control a nuclear arsenal.

A year later, in 1961, Soviet dominance over Germany in the aftermath of the Germany's defeat in World War II led to

Russian leader Nikita Khrushchev, shown here, was known for his fiery language.

the construction of the Berlin Wall, which separated Communist East Berlin from West Berlin. The Communists claimed that the wall was constructed to keep the fascist west from infiltrating the Soviet Bloc, but in reality, it was built to prevent the mass exodus to the West of those living under Communist rule. In 1963, American president John F. Kennedy showed his solidarity with the Germans, saying that he took pride in the phrase, "I am a Berliner." The speech may have reassured Germans, but it did nothing to repair United States-Soviet relations: Khrushchev scorned it only days later.

Another iconic Cold War moment came, unexpectedly, during a hockey game. At the 1980 Winter Olympics, a group of American amateur hockey players was pitted against what was, by all accounts, the greatest team in the world: the mighty Soviet hockey team, a group of professional players who had pretty much decimated all opponents. In a stunning upset that was to shake up not only the sports world, but the world at large, the Americans defeated the Soviets, 4–3. As the game clock was ticking down to zero and it became increasingly apparent that spectators were witnessing one of the greatest upsets in sports history, American broadcaster Al Michaels was moved to ask his television audience if they believed in miracles. The moment transcended sports—for many Americans, it represented a miraculous cultural victory over the powerful Communist regime, which three years later, President Ronald Reagan would call an evil empire.

Ending the Cold War

A final iconic Cold War moment also occurred in Germany as American President Ronald Reagan visited the Berlin Wall in 1987. Soviet leader Mikhail Gorbachev had begun to oversee a softening of the Communist country's aggressive policies and cast himself as a man of peace, but Reagan was not convinced. Reagan seized the opportunity of his visit to Berlin "to raise East-West differences and questions about Mr. Gorbachev's commitment to ending the nuclear arms race and his internal liberalization policies."[1] Standing 300 feet (91 m) from the barrier that divided East and West Berlin, he said, "'Mr. Gorbachev, tear down this wall' … At the time, the Soviet news agency TASS called Reagan's visit to the Wall 'openly provocative, war-mongering.'"[2] Nevertheless, the wall's gates were opened in November 1989, and over the next year, the wall was gradually torn down.

How did relations between the superpowers get to the point where the Soviet Union and the United States were pointing missiles at each other, on the brink of World War III? How did the world get a resolution to the years of turmoil, so that by 1991, in his farewell address, Mikhail Gorbachev confidently asserted that "The threat of nuclear war has been removed"?[3] Now, in the early 21st century, as Russian and American affairs have become increasingly entwined, and as Vladimir Putin seeks to gain back some of the lost Soviet

The Berlin Wall separated East Berlin from West Berlin for almost 30 years.

Republics, what lies ahead for this relationship? To answer these questions, one must look back at the entire history of Russian-American relations, delve into their cultural similarities and differences, and consider the countries in the context of the world surrounding them.

CHAPTER ONE

EARLY RUSSIAN AND AMERICAN RELATIONS

Given the often hostile relationship between Russia and the United States today, it might be surprising to learn that such hostility was not always the case. As political scientist Charles E. Ziegler wrote, "American–Russia relations were quite friendly and productive before the twentieth century."[4] One historian, John Lewis Gaddis, went as far as to say that the bond between the two powers was "the most consistently friendly relationship the United States would have with a major European power in the nineteenth century."[5] It was not until the 20th century in general, and particularly after the Russian Revolution following World War I, that Russian and American interests began to diverge. In the 18th century, there was no formal relationship between the Russian Empire and the English colonies, as any Russian acknowledgement of America risked alienating Great Britain, with whom Russia was often at odds, even more so than with the United States.

Russia and the American Colonies

There are documented instances of an informal relationship between the Russian Empire and the American colonies. In 1763, a two-masted sailing ship, the *Wolfe*, owned by a Boston merchant, delivered to Russia "a cargo of sugar, indigo, rum, mahogany, and sassafras, all originating in the West Indies."[6] The ship returned from Russia to New England with "hemp, iron, and linen cloth."[7] This commerce between Russia and the colonies was in clear violation of the British Royal Navigation Laws, which forbade the colonies from engaging in commerce directly with countries besides Britain. According to Norman E. Saul, "The British governor of Massachusetts was put on guard to interdict [intercept] this shipping but with no apparent result."[8] Other ships from the colonies, including vessels from New York and Philadelphia, followed suit, demonstrating the colonies' desire to gain economic independence from their colonial power, the British Empire.

Communication between Russians and colonists took place on another, completely different, front. "This took the form of the acquaintance of M.V. Lomonosov and other Russian scholars with the works of Benjamin Franklin."[9] Franklin was a much admired figure in Europe, and Lomonosov, a scientist interested in the study of electricity, became familiar with Franklin's famous experiments in the same area. As a result of this correspondence, Franklin's reputation in Russia grew dramatically. The esteem that Russians hold for Franklin is borne out by their printing of a postage stamp celebrating the American statesman and inventor during the Cold War period in 1956.

Benjamin Franklin was admired by the Russians, and they printed a postage stamp with his picture on it during the tense Cold War period.

However, most communication between the Russian Empire and the colonies was indirect. The Russian monarchy was kept aware of rising tensions between England and its colonies by the Russian Ambassador in London, Count Aleksei Musin-Pushkin. However, the Russians, having been involved in their own peasant rebellion and at war in the South with the Ottomans, were in no position to take an active part in the growing conflict that would result in American independence.

Russia and the War for American Independence

Catherine the Great would play an interesting role in determining the outcome of the American Revolution, largely by remaining neutral. If Russia had been determined to interfere in the conflict, it could have changed the course of the war. As it was, Catherine was wary of aligning herself with the colonies, but she was equally reluctant to aid Great Britain. She had disdain for British monarch George III as a statesman and had

TWO GREAT EMPIRES

To observers of 18th century world affairs, one idea was becoming clear: Russia and the United States were gaining power. As early as 1777, American diplomat Silas Deane commented that "Russia like America is a new state, and rises with astonishing rapidity."[1] Three years later, Baron Melchior von Grimm wrote to Russian Czarina Catherine II (better known as Catherine the Great) that in the future:

> *Two empires will...share all the advantages of civilization, of the power of genius, of letter, arts, arms and industry: Russia on the eastern side, and America, having become free in our own time, on the western side, and we other peoples of the nucleus will be too degraded, too debased, to know otherwise than by a vague and stupid tradition what we have been.*[2]

Von Grimm, a German, suggested that Russia and the United States would come to dominate world affairs and leave behind the former European powers. He may have been flattering Catherine the Great, but his prediction was to be realized as future world events unfolded.

1. Quoted in Paul Dukes, *The Superpowers: A Short History*. New York, NY: Routledge, 2000, p.14.
2. Quoted in Dukes, *The Superpowers: A Short History*, p.15.

even less respect for his ministers. She believed that it was their mishandling of the colonies that had led to the rebellion. According to Frank A. Golder, in June of 1775, "she predicted that America would become independent of Europe 'even in my lifetime,' and a year later she wrote to a friend, 'The colonies have told England good-bye forever.'"[10]

In her dealings with the two antagonists, Catherine was driven by self-interest. After all, this was a monarch who had expanded greatly the boundaries of the Russian Empire, continued Peter the Great's drive to westernize and modernize Russia, and improved the Empire's standing among world powers.

Catherine the Great's neutrality during the American Revolution was good for the American colonies.

Both England and the United States, nevertheless, sought her favors. In 1775, the English petitioned Russia for infantry troops to be sent to aid the British in America. After some misunderstanding, wherein the British believed that the request would be granted, Catherine firmly turned them down. She wrote a letter of refusal to George III, offering him some unsolicited advice in how to handle the colonies, and "the matter was ended; England was humiliated and disgraced."[11]

England was obliged to stoop even lower. James Harris, the British envoy to Russia, on multiple occasions pleaded with Catherine, with whom he had a good relationship, for help in ending the conflict. Finally, in desperation, Britain offered Catherine and Russia a bribe. If the empress would help end the war by persuading France to withdraw and leave the colonies to their fate, the British would perhaps make a gift of "some territory in America or in the Indies."[12] Not only did Catherine refuse this offer, but she also leaked news of it to the French, ensuring that Britain would be embarrassed on the world stage.

The Russian Empire's rejection of British overtures pleased the colonies greatly. "We are not a little pleased to find from good authority that the solicitations, and the offers of the Court of Great Britain to the Empress of Russia have been rejected with disdain,"[13] George Washington wrote to the Marquis de Lafayette in 1779. As the highly regarded Russian historian Nikolai N. Bolkhovitinov wrote in his book about United States-Russian relations, "in noting the decisive refusal of Catherine II to conclude any treaty of reciprocal aid with England, Washington stressed that the Russian government justified its position in expressions marked by 'a generous regard to the rights of mankind.'"[14]

For their part, the colonies did not have much more luck appealing to Catherine than did the British. "Catherine neither liked nor disliked the Americans," Golder wrote. "She probably knew none of them personally, and cared little about their theories of government."[15] In 1780, the colonies named Francis Dana, a Harvard-educated Boston attorney, to the position of minister to Russia, and he traveled to St. Petersburg, Russia, in order to gain an audience with Catherine II, taking with him 14-year-old John Quincy Adams, son of the future president and a future president himself. Catherine never granted Dana an audience. During this period, Catherine had attempted to mediate a peaceful conclusion to the American Revolution, though neither the British nor the Americans found her terms favorable. In order to maintain the air of impartiality, she "could not receive any American functioning diplomatically until a peace had been signed."[16] Lacking the prestige of Ben Franklin, Thomas Jefferson, or John Adams, Dana made little progress on his mission. He did "gain entry into high Russian political circles,"[17] but, ultimately, his mission to coax the Russians to the colonial side was a failure. Finally, in 1783, Dana gave up and returned to America.

The Declaration of Armed Neutrality

Despite Dana's failure, Catherine did make several maneuvers during the war that favored the colonies. Chief among these was the Declaration of Armed Neutrality in 1780. England had by far the most powerful naval fleet during this era, and its dominance on the high seas was unquestioned. Britain used this power to intercept foreign ships that it believed were supplying the colonies with goods. The declaration stated that neutral countries such as Russia, the Netherlands, Denmark, and Sweden could trade with warring parties (such as the American colonies) without interference, except where arms and military supplies were concerned. The British were attempting to guard entire coastlines in order to keep supply ships away from the colonies, but the declaration stated that only individual ports could be blockaded. In order to enforce her decree, Catherine had Russian ships sent to the Mediterranean Sea, the Atlantic Ocean, and the North Sea.

CATHERINE THE GREAT'S REACTION TO REVOLUTION

While Catherine the Great's actual effect on the American fight for independence was minimal, the revolution, along with that in France in 1789, certainly had an effect on her, and Russia as well. Previously an enlightened monarch who had established a number of liberal reforms, particularly in education, Catherine became increasingly wary that the Russians, looking to America and France as models, might also try to overthrow their monarch. The execution of the French ruler Louis XVI in 1793, in particular, was a shot to all European monarchs, and "suddenly, every sovereign in Europe was on red alert."[1] Catherine abandoned many of the Enlightenment principles she once believed in, scrapped the liberal reforms she had promoted, and turned into a tyrant. "She [began] to tamp down on anything that might lead to sedition at home," historian Douglas Smith said, "so she [took] away the right to own printing presses for individuals" and instituted censorship, "which had not happened before."[2]

1. Biography.com Editors, "Catherine II Biography," Biography.com, updated April 27, 2017. www.biography.com/people/catherine-ii-9241622#synopsis.
2. Biography.com Editors, "Catherine II Biography."

In the Declaration of Armed Neutrality, the Russian Empire made a powerful statement about freedom on the high seas. According to Norman E. Saul, "the Declaration [contained] at its heart the basis of modern maritime law regarding neutrality at sea."[18] Regarding the importance of the document to America, Nikolai N. Bolkhovitinov wrote that in circulating the Declaration of Armed Neutrality, "the Russian government vindicated … one of the principles in whose name the rebellious colonies in America were fighting. It is therefore not coincidental that many years later President James Madison wrote of Armed Neutrality as 'an American doctrine.'" Madison further wrote that the statement ushered in "an epoch in the history of maritime law,"[19] and that the United States would have an interest in upholding it.

Russians helped greatly in freeing the American crew of the Philadelphia *warship, which is shown here in this artist's interpretation.*

The Declaration of Armed Neutrality led to the formation of The League of Armed Neutrality. This league ultimately included Denmark, Sweden, Prussia, Austria, Portugal, and more. The league did little to change Britain's attitude concerning neutral shipping. However, it placed Britain in the position of being at odds with most of Europe and enabled trade with America that boosted both the colonies' morale and their ability to continue the armed conflict with a superior force.

When Catherine died in 1796, her son, Paul I, became the next Czar. When he was assassinated, Czar Alexander took his place, and a new chapter in Russian-American relations, with America now as an independent, self-governing nation, began.

Early 19th-Century Relations

Although normal diplomatic relations between the United States and the Russian Empire would not be achieved until 1809, the United States opened a consulate in St. Petersburg, Russia, in 1803. Already, initially as a result of the Declaration of Armed Neutrality, trade between the Empire and the United States had picked up. It would continue to grow during the 19th century. A U.S. warship, the *Philadelphia*, had been seized by pirates, and the Russians had assisted in freeing the American crew. Thomas Jefferson used this action as an opportunity to open relations by thanking Czar Alexander for Russia's help. Alexander replied warmly that he was glad to be of assistance, especially if it personally pleased the president. Thus, communication between the leaders of the two nations began in a friendly manner.

This resulted in the formal Russian recognition of the United States. In 1809, President James Madison selected John Quincy Adams as the first United States Minister to Russia. However, these were complicated times. Russia would soon find itself fighting with England against Napoleon, who attacked the Russian Empire unsuccessfully in 1812, and the United States would again find itself at war with England. Russia had to walk a fine line between staying friendly to both the United States and Britain. In order to do so, Russia once again tried brokering a peace between the two, as Catherine had attempted during the American Revolution. The United States accepted the mediation proposal, but England refused. However, Russia's attempted intervention placed Britain in the role of "bad guys" and positioned America well when Britain finally did sit down for peace talks and the two countries ultimately signed the Treaty of Ghent, ending the War of 1812. With Napoleon failing to conquer Russia, some semblance of peace and prosperity was restored to both America and Russia.

Russians in America

It is well-known that in the 19th-century, the Russians owned the territory now called Alaska. It is less well-known that Russians also settled in parts of the Northwest—in Washington State, Oregon, and as far south as Northern California. This idea, of course, clashed greatly with the American concept of Manifest Destiny, the idea that the entire continent was one day to be absorbed by the United States of America. One might think that this clash would have caused a major international incident, but the United States and Russia settled the issue of North American territory in a mostly cordial manner.

In 1799, the Russian-American Company had been organized to take advantage of the Pacific Northwest's resources, specifically with regard to developing the fur trade in the region. The company established headquarters in Sitka, Alaska, and expanded as far south as San Francisco, California. In 1812, they built a military outpost in northern California in what is now Fort Ross. However, their possessions were often raided by American trappers and traders. In 1821, Czar Alexander I issued a decree that forbade foreigners from using Russian-American land. This decree clashed with the American concept of Manifest Destiny, and John Quincy Adams, now U.S. secretary of state, wrote a forceful protest to the Russians. The scenario might have led to armed conflict, but Alexander never enforced the decree. Instead, he agreed to joint discussions with the United States and Great Britain to set territorial limits. These talks resulted in treaties that established a southern Russian border and allowed free trade in the Pacific Northwest.

However, the Russian's desire to expand in America had dwindled, and the U.S. government knew that it had. Russia was more concerned with protecting its European expansion, and the United States was more worried about English colonization of the Northwest. It is commonly believed among American historians that James Madison's Monroe Doctrine of 1823 (which stated that the United States would not tolerate any further colonization of the Americas by European powers), was aimed at Russian expansion into America. However, some Russian historians disagree and state that Madison was more interested in holding off England and France than Russia. Russian-American relations remained friendly during this period, leading up to the first agreement on trade and navigation in 1832.

This agreement provided American and Russian citizens with bilateral trading rights as well as most-favored nation treatment. This meant that the countries could trade free of tariffs, import quotas, and other trade barriers. Additionally, Russians and Americans were now able to trap, hunt, fish, and otherwise earn a living off the others' lands. While this agreement was mutually beneficial, some historians believe that it favored Americans.

Alaska, shown here, was once a Russian territory.

The Civil War and the Alaska Purchase

As in the case of the American Revolution, the Russian Empire did not have a direct role in the American Civil War. However, once again, the Russians did make their presence felt in an American conflict, and once again, they sided with the United States—this time against the Confederacy. Both Great Britain and France stood to make gains in North America if the Confederacy defeated the Union. France relied heavily on southern cotton, and Great Britain's rivalry with the official U.S. government was longstanding, dating back to before the American Revolution. The English also resented northern interference in their trade with the South. Russia also did not care much for the British and French, who had recently defeated the Russian Empire in the Crimean War. However, Russia avoided direct involvement in the Civil War.

Alexander II, now Russian czar, rejected British and French proposals to intervene in the war. He also refused to

The Russian Empire sold Alaska to the United States in 1867.

formally recognize the Confederacy. In 1863, an insurrection broke out in Poland against the Russian Empire, and France invited the United States to join them in fighting the Russians. Though sympathetic to the Polish, the United States refused, citing their non-interventionist policy in Europe and also the idea that they would be joining in a fight against the Russians.

Russia's sale of Alaska to the U.S. government in 1867 further illustrates the friendly nature of their relationship. However, it also signaled the Russian Empire's decision to focus expansion on Eurasia. There were numerous solid reasons for Russia to part with Alaska: The Empire had been weakened as a result of the Crimean War, the Russian-American Company was increasingly unprofitable, and Alaska was vulnerable to a potential English takeover. American Secretary of State William Seward was initially criticized for handing over $7.2 million for the sale, but he was later forgiven because of the discovery of gold in the Yukon region of Alaska.

Declining Relations

Most historians agree that the Alaskan agreement marked the high point of Russian-American relations in the 19th century. From this point forward, relations between the two emerging superpowers would decline all the way up to the period of the Russian Revolution. There were two major issues that divided the countries in the late 19th century: the treatment of Russian Jews and the controversy over Manchuria, a large region in Northeast Asia that borders Southeastern Russia. The first issue was a moral one, while the second involved trade and power.

Russian pogroms (organized attacks) against the Jewish minority had started as early as 1821 but picked up in frequency and intensity in the 1880s. Americans, especially American Jews, were disturbed by these vicious assaults on a minority, but the Russian government pointed out that America could hardly claim the higher moral ground. After all, blacks, Irish, and Asians were all victims of harassment and inferior societal status in 19th-century America. However, neither country could claim a morally superior position—both countries had relied heavily on forced labor. Russian serfs

Due to Russian pogroms, many Jews, such as those pictured here on the East Side of New York City, came to the United States.

were finally freed by Czar Alexander I in 1861, and Abraham Lincoln issued his famous Emancipation Proclamation a year later.

Nevertheless, Americans were hearing more and more about human rights violations in Russia and began to pressure the government into action. In addition to ill-treatment of Jews, Americans were told of the horrendous treatment of political prisoners in Siberia. In 1891, George Kennan, a traveler, writer, and lecturer, published *Siberia and the Exile System*, which detailed the abysmal conditions in Siberian labor camps and horrified American readers. However, it was the Jewish pogroms that had more of an effect on relations between the two countries, as Jewish emigration from Russia to the United States exploded. Wealthy Jewish magnates such as Jacob Schiff urged the United States to act to curtail the human rights abuses. The result of such entreaties was that the U.S. government annulled the 1832 treaty governing trade and navigation. The Russians were not pleased by this aggressive act, and it is seen by some historians as the first contributing factor in the deterioration of Russian-American relations.

RUSSIAN SHIPS SAIL TO AMERICAN PORTS

Grateful for American loyalty, the Russians sent fleets of ships to ports along the Atlantic and Pacific coasts of the United States in 1863. The Russians were greeted warmly by the North. Crowds of people turned out to cheer their arrival. As usual with the shrewd Russians, there was an ulterior motive: The Empire did not want their fleet to be stuck in Russian ports. The U.S. ports would give them a convenient base from which to sail if need be, especially if war broke out with the French and English over Poland. The Russians' actions likely had little decisive effects, either on the Polish or American conflicts. However, the British and French were well aware that a Russian-American alignment could change the balance of power in the world.

The Manchurian Controversy

The second divisive issue of this period, that of Manchuria, was a struggle over power and money. Nearing the turn of the century, the Russian Empire desperately wanted a warm water port because Russian ports were iced-in during the harsh winters. Their attempt to gain such a port in the South failed when they were defeated in the Crimean War. To gain a port in the East and to further their expansionist ambitions in Asia, the Russians, with Chinese permission, began building the Trans-Siberian Railway through Manchuria. The railroad would ultimately stretch more than 5,700 miles (9,173 km) from Moscow to Vladivostok on the Pacific Ocean. Russia's intention was to use Vladivostok to compete with British trade and naval might. However, when China became preoccupied with the Boxer Rebellion in 1899, Russia took advantage and occupied the whole of Manchuria. The Japanese, who had their own designs on Asian conquest, and—to a lesser extent—the United States both felt threatened. The United States believed that the Russians might shut out U.S. influence in the Far East. The episode was overblown, at least on the American side, and some historians saw the controversy as test of America's power. In 1902, the United States formed an alliance with Japan against the Russians but never had any serious intentions of going to war with Russia. Japan was another matter. On the night of February 8, 1904, Japan launched a sneak attack on the Russian Far Eastern fleet. A succession of Japanese victories followed, until President Theodore Roosevelt was able to broker a peace treaty in 1905 that confined the Russians to northern Manchuria.

The episode made the Russians bitter. They felt that the Japanese would not have pursued what is now called the Russo-Japanese War without the quiet approval of the United States and England. Moreover, the Russian persecution of Jews ended up playing a role in the war with Japan. Jacob Schiff, the American financier, actively discouraged loans to Russia by powerful banking interests. Their ability to finance the war was curtailed, and they ended up getting defeated by the Japanese. Russia had now lost two territorial wars in the past half century, and the biggest war of all was looming.

CHAPTER TWO

WORLD WAR I, THE RUSSIAN REVOLUTION, AND THE AFTERMATH

The period between 1914 and 1922 was one of tremendous upheaval in Russia. The Russians would find themselves enmeshed in World War I, involved in a political revolution that overthrew the czarist system permanently, and, finally, toward the end of this period, embroiled in a civil war. These events would alter the course of European—and world—history. Russia would emerge as a Communist dictatorship, and Europe would inevitably head toward a second world war. Despite its announced policy of avoidance of foreign entanglements (of which President George Washington warned in his farewell address), the United States would find itself inevitably drawn into European—and Russian—affairs. The end result was that by the end of the Russian Civil War in 1922, the United States and the new Soviet Union (as it was called from 1922 until 1991) would find themselves no longer "distant friends," but instead, philosophical and political adversaries.

The Great War

The key event in early 20th century Russian history, the revolution of 1917, might have eventually occurred without World War I, but the poor performance of the Russian Empire during the war undoubtedly triggered the revolution. Russia entered the war in August 1914. The war pitted Germany, Austria-Hungary, and the Ottoman Empire (often referred to as the Central Powers) against Great Britain, France, Russia, Italy, and Japan. The "war to end all wars" saw carnage on an unprecedented scale, largely due to new technology such as gas warfare, machine guns, and fighter planes. By the end of the war in 1919, a significant percentage of Europe's young men had died.

The war was fought on two fronts. Germany invaded France along what is now known as the famous Western Front, and Russia attacked Prussia along the less well-known Eastern Front. In August 1914, Russian troops were confronted by the Germans in what is now Poland. In what was to be a mismatch, the Germans defeated the Russian army. Nevertheless, by virtue of fighting the Germans on the Eastern Front, the Russians drew German troops and supplies that might have strengthened their Western Front. Over the next few years, the Russians mounted several offenses, attempting to break through German lines, but were no more successful.

The German army is shown here advancing on Russia during World War I. This war involved many other countries around the world, as well, including the United States.

As the war dragged on, the Russian army, at the time the largest in the world, grew dispirited. Russia's railway system was not sufficient to deliver needed supplies to the front. Additionally, Russia did not have the budget nor skilled leaders to wage an effective war. Many historians attributed the Russian army's losses to a lack of supplies, reporting that some soldiers were sent in to battle without arms, having been told there would be plenty of dead bodies from which to get a rifle. However, some historians reject this idea and see it as a tale that unskilled leaders made up in order to justify their defeats in battle. Additionally, many soldiers deserted the army, and there was poor organization.

Conditions were no better back home in Russia. Food was scarce, as was fuel. There were outbreaks of cholera and typhus. The peasants and poor workers, especially, suffered. Starvation set in, and many died. The Russian people focused much of their anger on Czar Nicholas II. He had not helped his cause by taking control of the Russian forces at the Eastern Front. Now, the people could blame Russia's failures directly on their leader.

The 1917 Revolution

In March of 1917, the people's anger intensified. "'The air is thick with talk of catastrophe,' U.S. embassy official Fred Dearing wrote in his diary, while American Leighton Rogers wrote that the city was 'like a taut wire'"[20] in St. Petersburg, which had been renamed Petrograd. The winter had been bitter cold, and women waited in bread lines for hours, sometimes only to be told that the shop had run out of bread. On International Women's Day, March 8, the cold weather broke, and temperatures rose. Women protesting the high price of bread flooded the streets, and workers from nearby factories joined them. Czar Nicholas ordered the Petrograd garrison of soldiers to crush the protest. However, the soldiers were reluctant to attack a crowd that contained so many women. The following day, after discussing the grave situation in their barracks, the soldiers joined the rebellion. Czar Nicholas II abdicated the throne on March 15 in favor of his brother, Grand Duke Michael Alexandrovich. However, Michael knew he would not have the support of the people any more than his brother did. He refused the promotion, and Nicholas II would forever after be known as the last Russian Czar. Because the Russians were still on the Julian calendar that was 13 days behind the standard, or Gregorian, calendar used in the United States and elsewhere, to this day, they refer to the uprising as the "February Revolution."

A provisional government, led by the Menshevik party, arose out of the ashes of rebellion, but it made many of the same mistakes as Czar Nicholas II did. In particular, the new government let the war drag on, and the

Workers' strikes, such as this one in 1917, were a feature of the Russian Revolution.

effects of the conflict—limited food and fuel, disease, economic collapse—all continued unabated. According to Richard Pipes, "The most striking aspect of the February Revolution was the extraordinary rapidity with which the Russian state fell apart. It was as if the greatest empire in the world had been an artificial construction, without organic unity. The instant the monarch withdrew, the entire structure collapsed in a heap."[21] By late April, Pipes continued, "the Provisional Government issued a pathetic appeal in which it conceded that it could no longer run the country."[22]

The Provisional Government's failure to alleviate Russia's ills left the door open for additional turmoil. A second revolution followed in October of the same year. The Bolshevik Party, later to be called the Communist Party, overthrew the Menshevik-dominated provisional government. Led by "professional revolutionaries" Vladimir Lenin and Leon Trotsky, the Bolsheviks proved more ruthless and authoritarian than the Mensheviks. Originally motivated by the socialist ideas of Karl Marx (author of *The Communist Manifesto* with Friedrich Engels), when they seized power, the Russian bourgeoisie (middle and upper-middle classes) became the enemy. The proletariat, or common people, were elevated, and the nobility was stripped of all privilege and possessions. It was the Bolsheviks who executed Czar Nicholas II and the rest of the Russian royal family, fearing that they could be used to motivate those who still favored a monarchy.

Vladimir Lenin, shown here, was the leader of the Bolshevik Party, which later became the Communist Party.

In August 1918, a revolutionist shot Lenin, wounding

him. In response, and in order to protect their political gains, Lenin and Trotsky oversaw a ruthless reign of terror similar to that which followed the French Revolution. This campaign of mass murder, torture, and oppression has gone down in history as "The Red Terror." As Richard Pipes wrote, "By 1920, Soviet Russia had become a true police state in the sense that the security police, virtually a state within a state, spread its tentacles everywhere."[23] The Bolshevik's deadly police force, called the Cheka, rooted out Bolshevik opponents wherever they found them. Pipes added that, "Estimates [of the Cheka's victims] range from 50,000 to 140,000. All one can say with certainty is that if the victims of the Jacobin [post-French Revolutionary] terror numbered in the thousands, Lenin's terror claimed tens of thousands of lives."[24] Once the Bolsheviks took power, they instituted a one-party state. The Communist party would rule Russia until 1991.

MARXIST COMMUNISM VERSUS RUSSIAN COMMUNISM

It is essential to understand that the practical "Communism" of Bolshevik Russia differed greatly from the philosophical communism originally adopted by Karl Marx and Friedrich Engels in *The Communist Manifesto* of 1848. According to Robert Daniels,

> *There is one essential point upon which the whole matter of the correct understanding of Communism rests. Contrary to every assertion, the Communist movement is not truly described by its doctrine … It can be shown beyond any reasonable question that within the terms of the Marxist picture itself, the … Communist movement does not occupy the place which its official spokesmen ascribe to it.*[1]

In other words, the Marxist philosophy, which advocates class warfare in order to promote a society in which all property is publicly owned and workers are paid according to their abilities and needs, has little to do with Russian Communism. The Bolsheviks may have started with the best of intentions, but their Communist experiment devolved into little more than a murderous dictatorship.

1. Robert V. Daniels, *A Documentary History of Communism in Russia: From Lenin to Gorbachev.* Hanover, NH: University of New England Press, 1993, p. xix.

Russia Makes a Separate Peace

The Bolsheviks also ended the war—at least, for the Russians. In 1917, as the United States was entering World War I, Russia was leaving the war. This was highly problematic for the Allies, who needed the Central Powers to be occupied on two fronts in order to dilute their strength. Under the Bolsheviks, Russia had unsuccessfully tried to end the war for all parties during peace talks at Brest-Litovsk. The terms were harsh. Russia had to cede vast portions of its western lands (Estonia, Latvia, and Lithuania) to appease the Central Powers. Given that the Bolsheviks had also granted Poland and Finland independence, Russian-controlled territory shrank to a fraction of its former self.

Russia's relief from leaving the war was America's burden. In short, the Allied powers felt betrayed by the Bolsheviks. They had supported the provisional government because they were happy to see Russia move toward what they thought would be a democracy—but it was easy to see, even from afar, that the Bolsheviks had no intention of promoting democracy. As Thomas A. Bailey wrote,

> *The legend took quick root, in ignorance of their immense sacrifices, that the Russians were cowardly quitters. "Trotsky might get the ignoble peace prize," jeered the Raleigh (North Carolina)* News and Observer. *[William Randolph] Hearst's Baltimore* American *[criticized] the work of "a group of lewd fellows of the baser sort: filthy pocket-pickers and despicable degenerates of lucre [money]."*[25]

U.S. public opinion strongly supported President Woodrow Wilson's refusal to formally recognize the new government. Just as Catherine II would not recognize the United States for many years after the Declaration of Independence, now, an American leader declined to acknowledge post-czarist Russia, or, the new Union of Soviet Socialist Republics (U.S.S.R.), as it called itself beginning in 1922. Americans still sympathized with the Russian people, and some even called for the United States to intervene. Unfortunately, the tyranny was only just beginning.

After the Russian surrender to the Germans, chaos ensued. The Bolsheviks had many enemies within Russia, particularly the overthrown upper class, and civil war soon broke out. The lines were drawn. On one side was the Red Army of Bolsheviks, supported by the proletariat. On the other was the White Army, supported by those who favored capitalism and the monarchy. To add to the confusion, a Green Army fought against both the Bolsheviks and the White Army.

The Bolsheviks proved to be tough. Under Trotsky's leadership, they fought ruthlessly, and for a cause. Lenin and his comrades did not just believe they were fighting for Russia. They believed that their brand of Communism would spread to the rest of the world, perhaps starting with Germany, whom they felt was withering under the kaiser's leadership and was ripe for a rebellion on the order of the Russian Revolution. The United States, as far as Lenin was concerned, was a capitalist enemy. In 1918, in his "Letter to American Workers," Lenin argued that America's gap "between the handful of arrogant multimillionaires who wallow in the filth and luxury and the millions of working people who constantly live on the verge of pauperism" suggested that the United States was no democratic nation founded on equality, but "the latest, capitalist stage of wage-slavery."[26] Given the abysmal conditions in American factories as depicted by socialist American writer Upton Sinclair in his novel *The Jungle*, where lives of those affected by "wage slavery" are dramatically detailed, there was some validity to Lenin's observations. Many Americans, particularly intellectuals, not wholly aware of the horrors of the Bolshevik regime, became intrigued by a Communist alternative.

American Intervention in Russia

American President Woodrow Wilson sent two groups of American soldiers into the chaos that was post-revolutionary Russia. The United States, despite its traditional isolationist stance, had been inevitably drawn into the European war. On April 6, 1917, after a series of German provocations, including the famous sinking of the *Lusitania* ship, Wilson declared war on Germany. The United States did not have a large standing army, but after the passage of the Selective Service Act in May 1917, millions of recruits were drafted. By 1918, the United States was sending 10,000 soldiers a day to the Western Front in France.

Far fewer, about 14,000 total, were sent to Russia, but Wilson believed the United States needed a presence there as well. With the Russians out of the war, it was still necessary to keep the Central Powers divided so that all the enemy attention would not be focused on the Western Front. One group of American soldiers was sent to Archangel, far in the North, and another to the cold wasteland of Siberia, in the East. Their missions may well have been doomed from the start, but Wilson had several more good reasons for sending American troops to Russia. In particular, despite not actively fighting the war, the Americans had sent almost $1 billion in armaments to the Russians. Now that the latter were out of the war, Wilson worried that the weapons would fall into the wrong hands. There were other reasons—Wilson feared that Japan was again making inroads into Manchuria and might come to dominate the region in the chaos of the Russian Civil War. A third reason involved the Czechoslovak Legion, a force of more than 70,000 Czechoslovakian exiles and prisoners of war who had been fighting with the Russians against the Central Powers. With Russia out of the war, the Czech forces had begun battling the Bolsheviks, and Wilson thought that only American troops could ensure their free passage out of Siberia. A fourth reason for Wilson's actions is that he simply could not stomach the idea of the Bolsheviks running Russia. While American forces were under strict orders not to fight the Bolsheviks, they eventually did so anyway, suffering heavy casualties and ensuring the enmity of the Bolsheviks going forward. With war between the Red Army, the White Army, the Green Army, the Japanese, the Czechs, and forces from Britain, Canada, France, Italy, and China still in the country in the aftermath of the war along the Eastern Front, Russia was a mess.

Wilson's decision to send a modest amount of American troops did not help matters. During their stay in Russia, World War I ended, as the Germans surrendered and the Treaty of Versailles was signed on June 28, 1919, and so, one original job of the American troops, to shore up the Eastern Front in the absence of the Russian Army, no longer existed. Nevertheless, the American troops stayed until 1920. As Carl J. Richard wrote, "The Siberian intervention was a complete failure. In the beginning it failed to lead to the formation of a new Eastern Front; later it failed to cause the destruction of the Soviet government and to thwart Japanese schemes in Siberia and Manchuria."[27]

The First Red Scare in the United States

The United States initially looked favorably on the Russian Revolution, believing that a new, democratic Russia would emerge. However, once the Bolshevik, soon to be the Communist, Party took over, American hopes were quickly dashed.

From a distance, Bolshevik rule looked attractive to a small amount of Americans. American John Reed's famous book about the October Revolution, *Ten Days that Shook the World*, painted a positive picture for American readers. In 1919, the first American Communist Party formed. Events such as a strike of Seattle, Washington, workers and a Boston Police Strike in Massachusetts encouraged government fear of organized labor. In April 1919, anarchists (people who rebel against a government) mailed bombs to prominent politicians, including the attorney general of the United States, judges, businessmen such as John D. Rockefeller, and others.

The frenzy that followed has been labeled the first Red Scare, which lasted until May 1920. A second, much more well-known Red Scare would occur following World War II. This first Red Scare was fueled by an aggressive government response, media hysteria, and public fear. Thomas A. Bailey wrote, "The Red Scare was primarily a domestic disease, and more important as a manifestation of the overwrought emotionalism of the war [World War I] than as an incident in Russian-American relations. But it further seared into the American public mind the familiar stereotype of a bloodthirsty, bewhiskered, bomb-throwing, free-loving Bolshevik."[28]

U.S. Attorney General A. Mitchell Palmer, who hoped to get the 1920 Democratic nomination for president, used the Red Scare to his political advantage, aided by J. Edgar Hoover, who headed the newly created General Intelligence Division in the Justice Department and who would later head the Federal Bureau of Investigation (FBI). They gathered intelligence on thousands of radicals, deported some, arrested others (often without warrants), and housed the imprisoned in miserable conditions—so bad that inmates suffered from ill health and sometimes died. In short, their actions were not much better than those of the Bolsheviks they claimed to loathe. As Peter G. Boyle wrote,

> *The Red Scare of 1919-20 illustrated fundamental contractions in American attitudes towards Communism which run through the history of US-Soviet relations. On the one hand, it was logical and reasonable for the United States to be concerned by the threat of the world-wide expansion of Communism and by Communist subversion within the United States. On the other hand, it was illogical and irrational to meet this threat by measures which violated the ... civil rights of alleged radicals.*[29]

The Red Scare finally came to a halt in 1920. Attorney General Palmer had forecast a huge radical rebellion on May Day (May 1). There would be bombings, assassinations, and worker strikes, but nothing happened. Palmer's warnings were exposed as a hoax, and the Red Scare hysteria quickly dissipated. Even when an anarchist bomb exploded in October of that year, the public remained calm.

A Period of Nonrecognition

Fear of the Bolsheviks was a factor in the refusal of the United States to recognize the Union of Soviet Socialist Republics. After Vladimir Lenin's death in 1924, Joseph Stalin emerged as the Soviets' leader, effectively clearing the way by putting to death most of his rivals. Trotsky, for example, was exiled in 1929, but Stalin had him murdered in Mexico in 1940.

Russia was still suffering from the same problems that had plagued the country during the war, and Stalin put aside the Bolsheviks' goal of a new Communist world order to concentrate on an economic recovery. The United States generally despised the Communist leadership but had empathy for the Russian people. The American Relief Administration had supplied half a million tons of food and medical supplies to millions of Soviet citizens from 1921 to 1923. Ironically, this aided the Bolsheviks and allowed Stalin's reign of terror to continue.

COMMUNIST SYMPATHIZERS IN THE UNITED STATES

For those in the United States sympathetic to Communism, the Great Depression signaled the failure of capitalism. It was during this period that fascination with Communism reached a high point. According to Peter G. Boyle, "Propaganda was distributed through the American Communist Party. In the course of the 1930s party membership grew from 12,000 to 80,000 by 1939."[1] Communists infiltrated government, trade unions, and schools. Liberal intellectuals, in particular, were drawn to Communist philosophy and willing to overlook the practices of Stalinist Russia. Malcolm Cowley observed, "All through the 1930s, the Soviet Union … was not so much a nation, in the eyes of Western radicals, as it was an ideal, a faith and an international hope of salvation."[2]

Contrary to expectations, right-wing and mainstream Americans did not overreact to the Communist threat during this period. As Boyle pointed out, "There was less hysteria over Communism in America in the 1930s when Communist party membership was at its height and Communist penetration of government at its most extensive than at a later time in the Red Scare of the late 1940s and early 1950s when Communist influence was much less."[3]

1. Peter G. Boyle, *American-Soviet Relations: From the Russian Revolution to the fall of Communism.* New York, NY: Rutledge, 1993, p. 31.
2. Quoted in Boyle, *American-Soviet Relations*, p. 32.
3. Boyle, *American-Soviet Relations*, p. 32.

During the 1920s, economic contacts were the most significant ones between the Soviet Union and the United States. The U.S. government was still highly skeptical about the Union of Soviet Socialist Republics despite the end of the first Red Scare, but "US exports to the Soviet Union rose to $68 million by 1925, more than any other nation."[30] Katherine A.S. Siegel observed that "Soviet economic initiatives and the American response to them gradually contributed to legitimizing the Russian regime in Washington."[31]

In American government circles, there was always talk of granting such a powerful entity as the Soviet Union formal recognition, but it generally fizzled out. Continued Soviet propaganda in the United States, dispersed by American Communists who took their cues from Moscow, was a major impediment. So too was repayment of the enormous debt, more than $100 million, that the Soviet Union owed to the United States for aid given during the czarist and temporary government years. When Herbert Hoover, an anti-Communist, was elected to the U.S. presidency in 1928, all such talk dissipated.

It was only with the presidency of Franklin D. Roosevelt, that, in 1933, the United States granted formal recognition to the Soviet Union. Roosevelt saw Japan and Germany as greater threats than the Soviet Union. He did not fully trust Joseph Stalin but viewed him as something akin to a political boss who only wanted to hold on to power and who could be cooperative. With the Great Depression raging in the United States and Adolf Hitler threatening Europe, Roosevelt knew he might need the Soviets in the future. Ironically, United States–Soviet relations deteriorated throughout the 1930s. Roosevelt's recognition of Russia came with some conditions. Included among these was that the Soviet Union would cease its propagandizing in the United States and that they would begin to pay back the debt they owed. The Soviets did neither.

The American government was further outraged by Soviet actions when the Soviet Union signed the Nazi–Soviet Nonaggression pact in 1939, also called the Molotov-Ribbentrop Pact. The two countries agreed that neither would attack the other, and, in a secret protocol that the Allies only learned of years later, divided up parts of Eastern Europe for plunder. For example, Poland was to be split into German and Russian territories. It has been suggested that both Stalin and Hitler were scheming through this division of Poland. Stalin thought he was placing more Russian territory between himself and the Germans, while Hitler envisioned a path through Poland right into Russia. The Soviets drew further criticism when they invaded their former territory, Finland, in the Winter War of 1939 to 1940. Despite English, French, and American aid, as well as fierce resistance on the part of the Finns, the Soviets succeeded in overwhelming them, gaining back some of the territory lost when Finland became independent. However, Finland retained its sovereignty and its international reputation, and Hitler, sensing weakness in the Soviet Army, believed even more so that he could eventually go back on the Russian treaty.

CHAPTER THREE

WORLD WAR II

When Hitler attacked Russia in June 1941, many Americans felt that the United States should continue its non-interventionist tendencies and let two countries take care of their own issues. However, the Japanese attack on Pearl Harbor on December 7, 1941, forced the United States into the war, and just four days later, Hitler declared war on the United States. At that point, America had already been sending the Soviet Union massive amounts of aid, and Roosevelt proclaimed, "We must be the great arsenal of democracy."[32] In October 1941, the United States pledged $1 billion worth of supplies to Russia—and that was just for the next 9 months. Roosevelt saw Germany as the main threat and was willing to give aid to any country that opposed Hitler and Germany, even if the leader of that country was Stalin.

German soldiers are shown here firing a machine gun during the invasion of Russia.

After America's entry into the war, the United States "could assist the Russians openly and regularly, unhampered by the hypocrisy of neutrality." However, as Thomas A. Bailey wrote, "The blunt truth is that while the western American giant and the eastern Russian giant were in the conflict on the same side, they never became full-fledged allies either in spirit or in deed."[33] The Russians distrusted the United States possibly even more than the United States distrusted them.

Russia versus Germany

The aid was sorely needed. Despite numerous warnings, Stalin did not prepare the Russians for the Nazis' inevitable attack. Some historians have argued that Stalin was in denial: He could not envision the Germans breaking the Molotov-Ribbentrop Pact. Within days of the first invasion, the Soviet air force lay in ruins, their fleet of tanks was largely destroyed, and at least 1 million Soviet soldiers had been taken prisoner. It was rumored that Stalin sat in his country house, shocked, staring at a wall for a week.

The first German invasion of Russia in 1941 was three-pronged and highly ambitious: They aimed at St. Petersburg (renamed Leningrad) in the North, Moscow in the center, and the Ukraine in the South. They made remarkable progress, despite underestimating the vastness of the Soviet Union. By November, they had overwhelmed the Ukraine, had reached Moscow, and had laid siege to Leningrad, hoping to starve the population into submission. Some of the conquered peoples, such as the Ukrainians, who had been systematically and deliberately starved to death in the 1930s by Stalin, welcomed the German forces as liberators. However, Hitler considered these people only as subhuman slaves whose labor could benefit the Nazi war machine.

Historians estimate that as much as 40 percent of the Soviet Union was already under German control. Hitler counted on the Russians folding as quickly as the French. However, the Russian army, bolstered by propaganda that they were fighting for family and country, never gave up. As the winter set in, the German army understood what had defeated Napoleon more than 100 years earlier. They were unprepared for the bitter cold, and it took far too long for supplies to arrive from Europe. The Germans retreated more than 100 miles (160 km) from Moscow and regrouped, biding their time.

Hitler rewrote the German battle plan, with a focus on the city of Stalingrad, an industrial hub named for the Soviet leader. As such, it had great strategic and symbolic value. In July of 1942, the Battle of Stalingrad began. It was to be a turning point in World War II. Hundreds of thousands of Germans stormed the city, and despite fierce resistance from the Soviets, captured most of Stalingrad by October 1942. However, the Soviets were not finished. Under the leadership of General

Georgy Zhukov, a force of 1 million Russian soldiers massed outside the city. The Soviets had also used much of the past year to build armaments. When their Western lands had been attacked the previous year, Stalin had ordered a mass exodus of millions of Russians to the East, to the Ural Mountain region, and out of range of the Nazis. Factories had begun producing enormous amounts of weaponry and other equipment, some of it superior even to that which the Germans possessed. While aid from America and England helped the Soviets, Russians primarily used their own resources.

General Georgy Zhukov, shown here, was a Russian war hero. He was so important to the war that a monument to him stands in Moscow.

Zhukov's forces surrounded Stalingrad, cutting off any escape route for thousands of German troops in the city. By January 1943, the Germans in Stalingrad were defeated. In Mark Steinberg's words, "This was the turning point in the war … and not only the turning point for Russia, but, many have argued, for the entire Allied cause against Nazi Germany … From Stalingrad on, the German army was in retreat, and the Red [Soviet] Army was rapidly moving westward."[34] The Germans mounted one more offensive against the Soviets at the Battle of Kursk in July 1943, but here, too, they were overwhelmed. The Red Army would not stop until it reached Berlin.

The Rise of Communist Russia

The eventual victory over Germany was a source of national pride for Russia. Even more important, it was a statement to the world that the Bolshevik government set in motion by the October 1917 rebellion, and previously scorned by many in the West, was now a force to be reckoned with.

For years, Stalin had begged England to open another front in the West to dilute the Nazi forces. The Allies finally did so with the famous landing in Normandy, France, on D-Day, June 6, 1944. However, by this time, the Germans were already in retreat from the Eastern Front. These developments gave Stalin and the Russians the sense that they had largely defeated the Germans

The victory over Nazi Germany heightened Soviet prestige around the world.

on their own. To the Soviets, the long awaited and promised second front took so long to materialize that they believed that Russia was fighting the war alone and the Allies were just bystanders. Though this was clearly not the case, and though the British and Americans were fighting the Nazis in Northern Africa and Southern Europe, a large number of casualties on the Allied side were Russians. Allied aid, which reached $11 billion, bolstered the Soviet cause. The cause was also bolstered by intelligence the English provided once their cryptologists, led by Alan Turing (now immortalized in the movie *The Imitation Game*), cracked the German's famous Enigma Code. The Enigma was a machine the Germans used to send coded messages, such as military communications, securely.

However, the Russians were not wrong in believing that their system of government, their industrial strength, their generalship, and their national attitude had played a large role the Nazi downfall. In 1945, Russian troops entered Berlin, a city over whose East side they would not give up leadership until 1991. Their victory over Germany would give them leverage in all negotiations with the other Allies in the postwar era. Stalin believed that the invading Germans owed him much in reparations for the destruction they had caused in the Western Soviet Union, and he was prepared to stand up for the Soviets' right to exact monetary and territorial revenge on the Nazis.

Franklin Roosevelt and Britain's Winston Churchill were aware that Stalin would make demands—many of them unreasonable—should the war go the Allies' way. Knowing this, they met with the Russian leader, in a summit of the "Big Three," in Tehran, Iran, in November 1943, and in Yalta, Crimea, in February 1945. Each leader came with his own agenda. As a Communist, Stalin believed that the Nazis represented the ultimate in barbaric capitalism, and he had no great love even for his capitalist allies in the West. Churchill and Roosevelt, of course, wanted to promote democracy around the globe. Roosevelt was eager to get Stalin's Russia to join the newly forming United Nations, a body designed to promote peace and justice throughout the world. At issue was the political fate of all the countries that Nazi Germany controlled.

Negotiations and Their Aftermath

At Yalta, an ailing Roosevelt (who died only a couple of months later) met with Churchill and Stalin to determine the fate of postwar Europe. Roosevelt also desired that the Soviets aid in the campaign against Japan, which was still raging in the Pacific. Stalin agreed to do so but ultimately did not declare war until after the Americans dropped the atomic bombs on Hiroshima and Nagasaki. The leaders also agreed to divide Germany into four occupied zones to be controlled by their three countries plus France.

Winston Churchill (left), Franklin D. Roosevelt (center), and Joseph Stalin (right) are shown here at their meeting in Yalta.

Much of the arguments between the leaders rose over their differing plans for Poland. Churchill and Roosevelt favored a democratic-leaning government that was currently in exile in London, England. Stalin, however, desired a buffer zone between the Soviet Union and the West. His reasoning was not without merit: "Throughout history Poland has been a corridor through which the enemy has passed into Russia," he argued. "Twice, in the last 30 years our enemies, the Germans, have passed through this corridor ... Poland is not only a question of honor but also of life and death for the Soviet Union."[35] Stalin went along with Churchill's and Roosevelt's plan for free Polish elections, but it became clear soon after that he would not follow through on the agreement.

There are some historians who think that had Roosevelt not died, the Soviets

RESTORING THE SOVIET ECONOMY

For a brief period, there was hope that the United States and Russia could live in a peaceful, coexistent world. As Thomas A. Bailey wrote,

> *When the war ended with an atomic bang in 1945, the American people still retained a vast reservoir of good will toward their valiant Russian ally. He had saved their hides while saving his own. Not only were Americans counting on Soviet co-operation to create a warless world, but many of them favored lending Russia money and technical assistance to repair the ravages inflicted by the Nazi invader.*[1]

However, Stalin was not interested in working with the Americans. Fixated on protecting Russia from future incursions and on reconstituting his ravaged nation, he "brutally pushed aside the outstretched American hand."[2] Cooperation with the West would deter his Communist goals. Stalin was equally brutal with his own country. The former mass murderer, who had executed any of his countrymen who disagreed with him and who had deliberately starved millions in the Ukraine, returned to his savage ways in the name of restoring the Soviet economy. There are many historians who believe he would have unleashed a new reign of terror in the Soviet Union had he not died in 1953.

1. Thomas A. Bailey, *A Diplomatic History of the American People*. New York, NY: Appleton-Century-Crofts, 1958, p. 777.
2. Thomas A. Bailey, *A Diplomatic History of the American People*, p. 777.

and Americans would have had more of a chance to maintain a friendship. Thomas A. Bailey argued that the "Truth is that by mid-March 1945—one month before the President's death—the Soviets were clearly taking over Poland and Romania as satellites in violation of their solemn pledges at Yalta."[36] The Russians had only dropped their Communist ideology for the sake of presenting a united front with the other Allies during World War II. Once the threat of annihilation by the Nazis was removed, Stalin reverted to his Communist goals. American opinion toward the Soviets changed rapidly in the years after the war. Soon, many in the United States believed that war with the Soviet Union was imminent.

It did not help United States–Soviet relations that President Harry Truman, Roosevelt's successor, took a harder stance against Stalin. The United States felt a sense of military superiority after developing the atomic bomb, and it was not about to bow to any other government. On the eve of the Potsdam Conference in 1945, Churchill, Stalin, and Truman convened to decide how to deal with the now-defeated Germany. Truman said of the atomic bomb: "If it explodes as I think it will I'll certainly have a hammer on those [Soviet] boys."[37]

The destroyed Japanese city of Hiroshima is shown here. Some historians believe President Truman used atomic weaponry to send a message to the Soviets.

CHAPTER FOUR

THE COLD WAR

The Soviet Union and the United States clearly emerged from World War II as the world's dominant countries. The British Empire would no longer dominate the world, and the colonialism of other former European powers such as the French was beginning to be challenged. In his country's diminished state, Winston Churchill recognized the Soviet threat in a famous speech:

> *From Stettin in the Baltic to Trieste in the Adriatic, an iron curtain has descended across the Continent. Behind that line lie all the capitals of the ancient states of Central and Eastern Europe. Warsaw, Berlin, Prague, Vienna, Budapest, Belgrade, Bucharest and Sofia, all these famous cities and the populations around them lie in what I must call the Soviet sphere, and all are subject in one form or another, not only to Soviet influence but to a very high and, in many cases, increasing measure of control from Moscow.*[38]

Churchill went on to say that "The safety of the world requires a new unity in Europe, from which no nation should be permanently outcast."[39] Russian historians Nikolai Sivachev and Nikolai Yakovlev stated that "Churchill's speech called forth enormous indignation throughout the world," but this is from the Russian perspective, so the indignation might have been more precisely located in the emerging Soviet bloc. However, the "iron curtain" speech certainly angered Stalin. He responded,

> *As a matter of fact, Mr. Churchill and his friends in England and the United States are laying before the non-English speaking-nations something like an ultimatum: acknowledge our supremacy voluntarily, and then everything will be all right, otherwise war is inevitable … Beyond all question Mr. Churchill's aim is a war aim, a summons to war against the U.S.S.R.* [40]

Winston Churchill (right) is shown here with U.S. President Harry Truman.

The Soviets believed, with some justification, that the United States was holding the threat of nuclear warfare over the rest of the world, and America could use the atom bomb as a club with which to beat other countries into submission. "Only this can explain the astounding change in the view of the United States government about the possibility of cooperation with other nations as equals,"[41] Sivachev and Yakovlev asserted. However, such statements are more propaganda than history, for they ignore the Red Army's incursions into countries such as Poland, Romania, Hungary, and Czechoslovakia and the totalitarian regimes that military strength allowed Stalin to install. Certainly Stalin had good reason for creating a buffer zone between potential invaders and Russia, but his actions indicated that he seemed to want much more.

Containment

In Washington, D.C., the Truman administration was concerned. They had come up with two opposite ways to deal with the Soviets: One was to fight World War III, a possibility no

GEORGE F. KENNAN'S LONG TELEGRAM

Joseph Stalin confused American officials. They did not understand what he wanted or why he acted as he did. The State Department sent a request to a long-serving American diplomat, George F. Kennan, who was stationed at the American Embassy in Moscow. Could he explain the Soviet mindset? In response, Kennan wrote the famous "Long Telegram" to the U.S. State Department in February 1946. The missive was a highly insightful, shrewd analysis of Soviet conduct that linked Stalin's actions to Russia's czarist past.

Kennan explained that Russian policy was rooted in its history of authoritarianism, starting with the czars. Russian history, Kennan maintained, was one of expansionism, and the nation had always sought to protect its borders from invaders. Simply put, Russian leadership had always been paranoid about the outside world. Stalin, in particular, needed a hostile outside world in order to justify the harshness of his regime. Even if the West completely gave in to Stalin, laid down their arms, and granted him his every wish, he would suspect something and wonder what deviousness they were up to. The Russians would respond well to a show of force, Kennan argued. Kennan's long telegram was devoured by officials in Washington, D.C. His advice led the United States to develop its policy of containment toward the Soviet Union.

one except the strongest war hawks, or those who favor war, wanted. The second was appeasement, to let Stalin have what he wanted in the hope that he would not want too much. Europe had tried the latter strategy with Hitler in the 1930s. It did not work.

In a 1947 essay published in the journal *Foreign Policy*, Russian expert George F. Kennan laid out a strategy for a "long-term, patient but firm and vigilant containment of Russian expansionist tendencies."[42] Kennan believed that over time, Communism was unsustainable and that the Soviet Union would implode. As Peter G. Boyle pointed out, "The greatest difficulty for Americans in pursuing containment was the exercise of patience, which has never been an American virtue."[43] Nevertheless, this policy dominated American strategy toward the Soviets for the next 50 years.

The war had left both Russia and Western Europe devastated. Due to dying economies and food shortages, Communist ideas had begun to take root in countries such as Italy, France, Greece, and Turkey. The Soviet sphere of influence threatened to engulf all of Europe. When the British announced they could no longer provide military and economic aid to the Greek government, which was involved in a brutal civil war with Communist forces that America believed were supported by the Soviets, Harry Truman went before Congress in March 1947, attempting to rectify the situation. "I believe it must be the policy of the United States to support free peoples who are resisting attempted subjugation by armed minorities or by outside pressures,"[44] he stated. The result was the Truman Doctrine, which sent $400 million to Greece and Turkey so they might resist Communism.

World War II had ushered in a great transition in U.S. foreign policy. America could no longer afford to pursue isolationism. The Truman Doctrine signaled that U.S. involvement in Europe would continue. Given the decline of the British Empire, the United States would take over as the leading supporter of democracy throughout the world. The United States had traded isolationism for internationalism. They were now a central actor in world affairs. It is a role the United States has not given up to this day.

In the aftermath of World War II, the United States implemented other measures to counter the Soviet threat. Chief among these was the Marshall Plan, which gave American aid to European countries devastated by the war. Billions of dollars were offered to all European countries as long as they used the money to purchase American goods and resources that would enable them to get back on their feet. Money was even offered to the Russians, who refused. They saw American aid to Europe as a threat. The Americans disagreed. As George C. Marshall, author of the plan, stated, "Our policy is directed not against any country or doctrine but against hunger, poverty, desperation and chaos."[45]

While Congress was debating the plan, Communists overthrew the government of Czechoslovakia. Funding was then approved. The Marshall Plan directed $17 billion in aid to Western Europe and "provided nets for Flemish fishermen, money to rebuild Italian automotive factories, construction equipment for France, and coal, to fuel Danish industry. The Marshall plan was an overwhelming success."[46] American aid put Europe on the road to recovery, fended off the spread of Communism, and established the United States as the world's dominant economic force.

The Marshall Plan was so successful in rebuilding Europe that it caused the Soviets concern. Stalin was especially aggrieved that Germany was making great economic strides. Russia controlled one-quarter of occupied Germany, and the city of Berlin was entirely within that sector, even though Berlin was also divided into four zones. In 1948, the creation of a new German currency, the Deutsche Mark, was the Soviet's tipping point. In order to weaken the non-Soviet sectors of the country, they blockaded all routes in and out of Berlin, so that even the non-Soviet areas of the city were cut off. In response, the democratic powers began flying over Berlin and dropping supplies to the Berliners. The Berlin Airlift was successful, and the Germans pulled the blockade a year later.

The World Chooses Sides

The Berlin Blockade was a catalyst in the formation of the North Atlantic Treaty Organization (NATO) in 1949. Led by the United States, NATO put together a solid core of democratic countries that banded together to protect individual members in the case of a Communist attack. In addition to the United States, original members included France, Italy, the United Kingdom, Belgium, Iceland, Canada, Denmark, Luxembourg, the Netherlands, Norway, and Portugal. Greece joined in 1952, Germany in 1955, former Soviet Republics such as Estonia and Romania joined in 2004, and Montenegro joined in 2017. As of 2017, 29 countries make up NATO.

According to Thomas A. Bailey, threats of Communism created a revolution in U.S. foreign policy. Non-entanglement became entanglement. The United States had forsaken non-intervention with the Marshall Plan. It had reversed its non-alliance policy with NATO. It had adopted a wartime military budget during peacetime. It had done all of these things with reluctance but with the instinct of self-preservation. "The new American policies," Bailey wrote, "were actually authored more by the men in the Kremlin than by the men in Washington. The American people had hoped for a peaceful world after World War II, but the aggressions of the Soviets simply would not permit them to drop their guard."[47]

The Soviets viewed NATO as a threat. In response, the Soviets signed the Council for Mutual Economic Assistance (CMEA) in 1949, and the Warsaw Pact in 1955, formalizing the bond of the Soviet bloc of Communist countries. These included Poland, Bulgaria, Czechoslovakia, Hungary, and Romania.

Despite America's emphasis on containment, Communism spread to Asia, Latin America, and the Middle East. China fell to Communist control in 1949, which led to a Sino-Soviet alliance ("Sino" meaning China). In 1950, North Korea, with Soviet aid, invaded South Korea, backed by the United States. The bloody conflict ended with a truce in 1953, but North Korea remains a problem for America to this day.

Joseph Stalin, the towering figure in Soviet politics and policy from Lenin's death on, died in 1953. Nikita Khrushchev, who rose to power shortly thereafter, sought to distance the Soviet Union from his mass-murdering predecessor (though Khrushchev himself encouraged Stalin's purges) and pursued a policy called de-Stalinization. Briefly, the Cold War thawed.

However, Khrushchev soon went on the offensive. In 1956, he sent tanks into Hungary to crush a popular uprising. In 1960, the Soviet Union shot down a U.S. spy plane, the U-2. Pilot Francis Gary Powers was convicted of espionage but served fewer than two years of a ten-year sentence when the United States and Russia arranged a "spy-swap."

Two events during this period had an even more dramatic effect on U.S. history. The first was the Soviets' successful launch of Sputnik, an unmanned satellite that orbited the earth in 1957, and kicked off the Soviet-U.S. space race. The second was the Cuban Missile Crisis of 1962, which came closer to causing World War III than any other single event.

The Arms Race

Nuclear arms have become a fact of life that 21st-century Americans are aware of, but one that rarely causes severe angst. The same could not have been said during the Cold War. Fear of nuclear annihilation was a constant. Schools conducted "duck and cover" drills, a preventive measure against the effects of a nuclear explosion. Citizens constructed fallout shelters in their basements and backyards. In his Nobel Prize acceptance speech in 1950, the novelist and chronicler of the American South William Faulkner expressed universal fears in this manner: "Our tragedy today is a general and universal physical fear so long sustained by now that we can even bear it. There are no longer problems of the spirit. There is only the question: When will I be blown up?"[48]

There are historians who believe that Truman's deployment of the atomic bomb over Hiroshima and Nagasaki was aimed more at the Soviets than the Japanese. Future U.S. President Dwight D. Eisenhower, the commanding

Author William Faulkner, shown here, expressed the fears of many Americans in his Nobel Prize acceptance speech in 1950.

general of U.S. forces, worried greatly about using the atomic bomb on Japan:

> *I had been conscious of a feeling of depression and so I voiced ... my grave misgivings, first on the basis of my belief that Japan was already defeated and that dropping the bomb was completely unnecessary, and secondly because I thought that our country should avoid shocking world opinion by the use of a weapon whose employment was, I thought, no longer mandatory as a measure to save American lives.*[49]

Eisenhower believed that the Japanese were defeated even before the nuclear attacks and that they were just trying to find a way to surrender with minimal loss of face. His theory makes perfect sense, given that Japanese credo during the war dictated death before surrender. The Japanese felt only disdain for American prisoners of war, whom they believed had given up rather than making the decision to fight to the death.

As historian Gar Alperovitz, author of *The Decision to Use the Atomic Bomb and the Architecture of an American Myth* wrote, "It still surprises many Americans to think that there might be a relationship between the bombing of Hiroshima and diplomatic strategy towards the Soviet Union."[50] Alperovitz cited physicist Albert Einstein's statement that the bombing was the result of "a desire to end the war in the Pacific by any means before Russia's participation." Einstein went further in saying that "if President Roosevelt had still been there, none of that would have been possible. He would have forbidden such an act."[51]

Russians had their sights on territory in the Pacific, particularly warm water ports, for centuries. Had the Soviets entered the war against the Japanese, Stalin might have laid claim to swatches of the Far East in the same way he came to dominate Eastern Europe. As British physicist and Nobel Prize winner P.M.S. Blackett said, "the dropping of the atomic bombs was not so much the last military act of the second World War, as the first major operation of the cold *diplomatic* war with Russia."[52]

Though the United States had ended the war with a display of the most fearful and intimidating technology ever unleashed, its atomic superiority was short lived. A ring of spies, including Julius and Ethel Rosenberg and a German-born physicist, Klaus Fuchs, had passed atomic secrets to the Russians. "Soviet espionage directed at the Manhattan Project probably hastened by at least 12–18 months the Soviet acquisition of an atomic bomb."[53] The Soviet Union's first nuclear test on August 29, 1949, set off a weapon that was almost identical to an American prototype. From this point forward, a nuclear arms race between the two countries ensued. The Americans developed an even more powerful weapon, the hydrogen bomb, in 1952. The Soviet Union soon followed suit. It was not until both countries had a nuclear arsenal capable of completely annihilating the other and the means to deliver those weapons, such as missiles and submarines, that a true standoff was enabled. This standoff, called "Mutually Assured Destruction" (or MAD, for short) came to define both American and Soviet nuclear weapons policy during the later Cold War. Neither country could risk attacking the other directly, and so the Cold War came to feature numerous proxy wars fought in other countries, such as Korea, Vietnam, Nicaragua, and Afghanistan, between Communist and Capitalist forces.

The McCarthy Era

In the late 1940s and early 1950s, fear of Communism gripped America in a manner not seen since the first Red Scare of 1919. This second Red Scare, which dominated American politics during the period, came to be perpetrated largely through the efforts of one politically-motivated person, Senator Joseph McCarthy of Wisconsin. In 1950, McCarthy claimed that he had "a list of 205 [State Department employees] that were known to the Secretary of State as being members of the Communist Party and who nevertheless are still working and shaping the policy of the State

THE CRUCIBLE

Arthur Miller's play, *The Crucible*, had its first performance on Broadway in January 1953. *The Crucible* tells the story of John Proctor, a Salem, Massachusetts, farmer who in 1692, was accused of witchcraft along with a group of other Salem citizens. The accusers were a group of young girls who had been caught dancing and casting spells in the forest. Such actions were illegal in Puritan Massachusetts, and the girls attempted to escape prosecution by blaming their conduct on witches. They were asked to name names and did so. At the end of the play, some of the accused "witches" are put to death.

A "crucible," often used in chemistry, is a container in which materials are subjected to high temperatures. Salem, Massachusetts, is symbolically on fire during the play. Miller wrote *The Crucible* during the McCarthy Era as a metaphorical response to the witch hunts being conducted by the House Un-American Activities Committee. In an essay written much later for *The New Yorker*, Miller stated, "The more I read into the Salem panic, the more it touched off corresponding images of common experiences in the fifties."[1]

1. Arthur Miller, "Why I Wrote 'The Crucible,'" *The New Yorker*, October 21, 1996, p. 163.

Department."[54] Though the number of Communists McCarthy cited changed with each further reference he made to his list in subsequent days, and though he never produced any evidence for his assertion, his speech induced paranoia in the American public. For all the public knew, a Communist could have been working right next to them. McCarthy was not wrong about there being Communists in the United States. Many left-leaning intellectuals had flirted with Communist ideas since the Russian Revolution, but the vast majority were no great threat to the American way of life. McCarthy was ultimately condemned by the U.S. Senate but not before his technique of conducting political witch hunts (now called "McCarthyism") threw the United States into a state bordering on hysteria and chaos.

Senator Joseph McCarthy, shown here, was the key figure in the House Un-American Activities Committee's hearings.

A group of Congressmen in the U.S. House of Representatives, the House Un-American Activities Committee (HUAC), investigated allegations of Communist activity in the United States. The committee had been established in 1938 but came to the forefront in the early years of the Cold War. The group began to focus its efforts on high-profile leftists in Hollywood, and many writers, actors, and directors were subpoenaed to appear before Congress. Included in this group were Elia Kazan, who directed the famous movies *A Streetcar Named Desire* and *On the Waterfront*; Dalton Trumbo, a screenwriter and author of the anti-war novel *Johnny Got His Gun*; and Arthur Miller, a playwright who wrote *Death of a Salesman* and *The Crucible*. Not only did they have to answer whether they were ever members of the Communist Party, but they were also expected to name others they suspected of having Communist affiliations. Miller, who was married to the movie star Marilyn Monroe at the time, believed that the entire process was a partisan farce. He once told the story, on the television show *60 Minutes*, of how one congressman's lawyer had told him that if the congressman could have a picture with Marilyn Monroe, he would call off the whole thing. Miller refused and questioned how people in Hollywood, such as actors, directors, and playwrights, could possibly have an effect on national security in the United States.

Still, hundreds of supposed Communists were imprisoned as a result of the hearings. In addition, many of the Hollywood people who refused to name names were blacklisted afterward, meaning they could no longer work in the movie business. Their careers were ruined. Like the first Red Scare, the second gradually ended, especially after June 1954, when Joseph N. Welch, chief counsel for the U.S. Army, famously asked Joseph McCarthy, "You've done enough. Have you no sense of decency, sir, at long last? Have you left no sense of decency?"[55] However, the McCarthy era of politics had already done its damage.

The Bay of Pigs and the Cuban Missile Crisis

In the 1960s, Communism and Capitalism once again clashed in Cuba. For years, the country had been under the U.S. sphere of influence, and the ruler, General Fulgencio Batista, was a U.S.-backed dictator. When Fidel Castro led a revolution in 1959, he followed the Communist blueprint, stripping the bourgeoisie of land and property, even that of U.S. businesses. Middle- and upper-class Cubans fled, most to Florida. Though Nikita Khrushchev originally had no interest in Castro and viewed him with distrust, Castro struck a deal with the Soviets to trade Cuban sugar for Russian fuel.

President Dwight Eisenhower, Truman's successor in office, was highly concerned about a Communist country only 90 miles (144 km) from the United States. He authorized a secret invasion by Cuban exiles, who would attempt to overthrow Castro. The Central Intelligence Agency (CIA) trained 1,500 Cuban exiles for the mission and provided them with equipment and air support. However, the Cuban government was tipped to the invasion, and when the attackers landed in the Bay of Pigs on the southern side of Cuba in April 1961, the Cuban military quickly defeated them. Their army had not been surprised by the invasion, and ordinary Cubans had not risen up in revolt as the United States had hoped.

U.S.-backed attackers were quickly captured during the Bay of Pigs invasion.

By this time, John F. Kennedy was president. He had somewhat reluctantly given the go-ahead for the invasion, which had been an Eisenhower scheme. Despite being urged to do so, Kennedy would not send the U.S. military to support the Cubans, fearing that such a move would initiate a war with the Soviet-backed Cuban nation. According to Peter G. Boyle,

> *The disastrous episode left Castro in a much more strongly entrenched position, with the forces of Cuban nationalism behind him in repelling the Yankees and their lackeys. American prestige was dealt a severe blow by such a blatant violation of international law in attempting to overthrow by violence the government of a small neighbouring state and by the incompetence in the execution of the invasion.*[56]

The failed invasion had major consequences for U.S.-Soviet relations. The Soviets felt justified in what followed after America's aggression: "In view of the constant threat of American intervention, the USSR and Cuba … reached an agreement on placing powerful means of a defense in Cuba, including rockets and medium-range bombers,"[57] Sivachev and Yakovlev wrote. In fact, the Soviets had placed nuclear arms in Cuba. When a U.S. spy plane observed the missiles in October 1962, a 13-day showdown ensued. The United States demanded that the Russians remove the missiles, but the Soviets insisted they were only defensive.

The U.S. Joint Chiefs of Staff recommended to Kennedy that the United States attack Cuba to put an end to this outrageous act. Instead, Kennedy placed a naval blockade around Cuba to stop future arms shipments. A naval blockade is essentially an act of war, so Kennedy called it a "quarantine." Nikita Khrushchev denounced it as an act of aggression. Both sides were hoping to avoid a showdown, and secret negotiations proceeded between the countries. Nevertheless, a Soviet rocket took down an American spy plane, and soon after, an American ship sent depth charges exploding around a Russian submarine. Unbeknownst to the Americans, the Russian sub was carrying a missile with a nuclear warhead, and nearly used it. The world had never come closer to atomic war.

Finally, the Soviets agreed to pull the missiles out if America would pull its own missiles in Turkey and Italy and promise to leave Cuba in peace. A deal was struck, and the world was left intact.

The Domino Theory and Vietnam

Skirmishes between the Communist East and the Capitalist West continued to crop up all over the world. The Bay of Pigs had briefly made the United States seem an inept laughingstock, but it had recovered some prestige in the aftermath

THE MAN WHO SAVED THE WORLD

Vasili Arkhipov is certainly not a household name, but perhaps he should be. If classified documents released in 2002, 40 years after the Cuban Missile Crisis, are accurate, Arkhipov single-handedly stopped a thermonuclear war.

On October 27, 1962, a U.S. naval destroyer located a Soviet Foxtrot-class submarine off the coast of Cuba that had gotten through John F. Kennedy's naval blockade. Seeking to force the sub to surface, the U.S. ship dropped depth charges that exploded around the submarine.

The officers in the submarine, which was too deep to communicate with the world above, believed the war had begun. In order to launch a nuclear missile, all three of the sub's top officers had to sign off. Two agreed, but Arkhipov did not. Because of his courageous decision, World War III was averted. Arthur M. Schlesinger Jr., a former Kennedy aide, said, "This was not only the most dangerous moment of the Cold War. It was the most dangerous moment in human history."[1]

1. Quoted in Marion Lloyd, "Soviets Close to Using A-Bomb in 1962 Crisis, Forum is Told," *The Boston Globe*, October 13, 2002. www.latinamericanstudies.org/cold-war/sovietsbomb.htm.

of the Cuban Missile Crisis. Many in Russia felt that the Soviet military had come off looking weak after the Missile Crisis. Several high-ranking Russian officers insisted that the captains should have used their weapons against U.S. ships. The reputations of both powers would continue to rise and fall during the remainder of the Cold War.

The U.S. military reputation took its biggest hit with the Vietnam War. Vietnam, formerly called Indochina, had been a French colony until breaking away. Ho Chi Minh, the leader of the North Vietnamese, had announced the founding of the Communist Party in Vietnam in 1930, with a stated goal of overthrowing "French imperialism, feudalism, and the … Vietnamese capitalist class."[58]

Vietnam's alignment with the Soviet Union worried U.S. officials. In addition to the policy of containment, the domino theory also guided American foreign policy during the Cold War. The domino theory held that if one nation fell to Communism, nearby countries might also topple, the way lined-up dominoes knock each other over. On April 7, 1954, President Dwight D. Eisenhower gave voice to the theory in describing his Indochina strategy: "You have broader considerations that might follow what you would call the 'falling domino' principle. You have a row of dominoes set up, you knock over the first one, and what will happen to the last one is the certainty that it will go over very quickly. So you could have a beginning of a disintegration that would have the most profound influences."[59]

Attempting to avoid that disintegration, the United States had sent military advisors to South Vietnam in 1950. The North Vietnamese (NVA) and the Viet Cong, South Vietnamese insurgents, fought against the South Vietnamese government and the United States in an attempt to reunite the country under a Communist government. The war escalated throughout the presidencies of Eisenhower and John F. Kennedy, then intensified under Lyndon B. Johnson. By 1967, approximately half a million U.S. troops were in Vietnam.

The United States believed initially that this war would not last long. It had overwhelming manpower and technology. However, the Vietnamese opponents had the advantage of the jungle terrain, guerrilla warfare, and a complex system of underground tunnels. In addition, they were not really fighting for Communism; they were fighting for their homeland, and this gave them motivation that a foreign attacking force such as the United States did not have. As Ho Chi Minh wrote to Lyndon B. Johnson, "The Vietnamese people deeply love independence, freedom and peace. But in the face of U.S. aggression, they have risen up, united as one man, fearless of sacrifices and hardships."[60]

The North Vietnamese were aided by the Soviets. They believed that America's involvement in Vietnam was "a classic case of capitalist imperialism and American expansionistic aggressiveness."[61] For years, the Soviet Union denied participating in the war, but declassified information has shown that 3,000 Soviet troops fought in Vietnam. "Soviet expertise played a vital part in training Vietnamese forces, and Soviet anti-aircraft missiles inflicted heavy damage on American planes."[62]

The war took its toll on the United States. Television news broadcast images of horrific violence to shocked Americans. Protests, particularly on college campuses, grew in size and intensity. Lyndon B. Johnson declined to run for a second term, and Richard Nixon, who promised that he had a "secret plan" to end the war, became president. There was no plan, and Nixon was unable to achieve his stated goal of peace with honor. The United States withdrew its forces in the first year of Nixon's second term. However, the Soviets and Communist China maintained their support of North Vietnam. U.S. government officials claimed that these two powers "had poured $1.7 billion of military aid into North Vietnam in 1974 alone."[63] In 1975, with Nixon, under threat of impeachment, out of office, the North Vietnamese overran the South and unified Vietnam under Communist rule. The United States had suffered a shameful defeat.

America's domino theory fears were overstated. Not only did neighboring countries not fall to Communism, but by the mid-1980s,

> *Vietnam's Communists conceded economic defeat ... and brought in market-based reforms called* doi moi *(renewal), similar to those [Chinese leader] Deng Xiaoping had introduced in China ... As in China, it took time for the effects to show up, but ... economic liberalization has been fostering rapid, poverty-reducing growth.*[64]

By the 21st century, America's war to defeat Communism in East Asia seemed unnecessary. Vietnam ultimately made peace with the United States and has remained on friendly terms. In 2007, Vietnam even joined the World Trade Organization, which promotes free trade around the globe. Russia did not join until 2011.

Thousands of Soviet troops assisted in the Vietnam War. A Russian advisor is shown here instructing a North Vietnamese student pilot in a Soviet fighter jet simulator.

Détente and Afghanistan

In the 1970s, Nixon sought to de-escalate hostilities between the Soviets and America through a policy now known as détente. Nixon became the first sitting president to visit the Soviet Union since the beginning of the Cold War. Détente had the effect of increasing trade and communication between the two superpowers. It also led to the Strategic Arms Limitation Talks (SALT) treaty to limit nuclear weapons. Presidents Gerald Ford and Jimmy Carter generally followed the détente policy. In 1979, Carter met with new Soviet leader Leonid Brezhnev to work out the details of a further reduction of arms called SALT II, but the treaty was never ratified by the U.S. Congress.

Détente ended with a boom in 1979 when the Soviet Union invaded the nation of Afghanistan in the Middle East. The Socialist Afghani government was on friendly terms with the Soviets, but Islamic forces, called mujahideen, believed that the Soviet Union's influence threatened their way of life. The mujahideen attacked government officials and the military. In December 1979, thousands of Soviet troops entered Afghanistan in support of the pro-Soviet government.

The war raged for almost 10 years. In many ways, it was a mirror image of Vietnam. This time, the Soviets were engaged full-scale in the conflict, and the Americans were sympathetic to the mujahideen opposition. This time, the United States believed that the Soviets were aggressively trying to bring territory under their influence.

As a result of the Soviet aggression, the United States and many other nations boycotted the 1980 Moscow Olympics. Four years later, the Soviets returned the favor as the Soviet bloc boycotted the Olympics in Los Angeles, California.

The United States sided with the mujahideen, but support was limited until a little-known Texas Congressman, Charlie Wilson, secured funds to supply the rebels with surface-to-air, handheld rocket launchers that were capable of neutralizing Russian air attacks. The war began to turn from that point forward.

Members of the mujahideen went on to form the hardline religious group the Taliban, and al-Qaeda, the terrorist organization behind the attacks of September 11, 2001. The Soviets ultimately withdrew in defeat from Afghanistan in 1989, as the Cold War was coming to an end.

CHAPTER FIVE

THE END OF THE COLD WAR AND THE RISE OF VLADIMIR PUTIN

U.S. President Ronald Reagan took office in 1981 and soon set his sights on the Communist enemy. Historians continue to debate Reagan's role in ending the Cold War and the demise of the Soviet Union. Reagan ramped up production of weaponry in his first term, spending as much on defense as Ford, Nixon, and Carter combined. He also ramped up the criticism of Russia, which he termed "the evil empire." As Peter G. Boyle wrote, "His harshly anti-Soviet speeches were needlessly provocative and helped to create the unhealthy mood of panic and fear in the early 1980s."[65]

In 1984, he stated that the United States would start bombing within minutes. His supporters took it as the joke he meant it to be; his detractors were horrified. His 1983 "Able Archer" war games in Europe were so realistic that the Soviets mistakenly believed he was starting a conflict and came close to retaliating.

Reagan's signature military triumph was to be the Strategic Defense Initiative (SDI), which received the nickname "Star Wars," after the blockbuster 1977 movie. This scheme would place missiles and lasers both on the ground and over the earth that would shoot down any incoming missiles—Soviet or otherwise. The problem was that the system was not practical. It was never built, though the technology developed at that time has led to the development of today's anti-ballistic missile systems. Reagan was wedded to SDI, however, as a means toward eliminating Mutually Assured Destruction and making America safe.

In response, the Soviets, who had a much weaker economy, increased their own military spending, to the detriment of the rest of the national budget. In short, the same type of economic woes that doomed Czar Nicholas II and the Mensheviks led to the demise of the Soviet Union.

Ronald Reagan is shown here addressing Germans at the Berlin Wall in 1987.

The End of the Soviet Union

In the United States, Reagan is often credited with ending the Cold War. This is a simplification. Most historians believe it was the 1985 ascension of Mikhail Gorbachev to the head of the *Politburo* (the executive committee of the Communist Party) that really foretold the end of the Soviet Union. The forward-thinking Gorbachev instituted dramatic, radical reforms, including *perestroika* and *glasnost*. *Perestroika*, or restructuring, was the reorganization of the Russian economic and political system. *Glasnost* suggested openness. Gorbachev eased the strict social controls imposed by the Communists. He allowed greater freedom to the media and religious groups and permitted citizens to express themselves. Gorbachev also steered Russia toward democracy, instituting an elected form of government.

Gorbachev's reforms did not solve the country's economic woes. It was said that Gorbachev was more popular abroad than in his own country. As a result of *perestroika*, Russia's restructured economy underwent drastic changes. An end to Soviet-era price controls, drastic cuts in state spending, and open foreign trade resulted in the devastation of the Russian economy. Millions of Russians plunged into poverty or saw their standard of living reduced. Corruption and organized crime exploded. Moreover, once it became clear that Gorbachev's military would not interfere in the revolutions of Soviet states, one after another, the former members of the Soviet Union declared their independence. "By 1991, the Soviet Union had collapsed into a loose constellation of 15 countries, including what became known as the Russian Federation."[66]

In August of 1991, a group of hardline Communist Party members attempted to depose Gorbachev and take control of the country. The coup failed, but it had dramatic effects. The Russian Federation rose out of the ashes of the old Soviet Union, as, on December 25, 1991, Mikhail Gorbachev resigned in favor of new leader Boris Yeltsin, and the red Soviet flag was lowered for the last time over the Kremlin and replaced by the tri-color, white, blue, and red Russian flag. In his resignation speech, Gorbachev stressed that the drastic changes in Russia were causing growing pains: "We haven't learned to use freedom yet."[67] Such words from a Soviet leader would have been unheard of only a decade earlier. Even more astounding in the context of Russia's long history was Gorbachev's summation of his accomplishments: "We opened up ourselves to the rest of the world, abandoned the practices of interfering in others' internal affairs and using troops outside this country, and we were reciprocated with trust, solidarity, and respect."[68] Unfortunately, Gorbachev's reforms were not to last.

Ronald Reagan (left) and Mikhail Gorbachev (right) oversaw the end of the Cold War.

EASTERN EUROPE'S COLOR REVOLUTIONS

After the collapse of the Soviet Union, governments in Eastern Europe were in a state of flux. Civil war and so-called "ethnic cleansing" (the attempted eradication of certain ethnic groups) occurred. Revolutions continued to break out in countries such as the former Yugoslavia, Georgia, Ukraine, Kyrgyzstan, Belarus, and Moldova. These periods of unrest, characterized by massive protests, often against rigged elections, have been labeled "color revolutions," as the demonstrations are typically accompanied by color symbolism, such as the Rose Revolution in Georgia or the Orange Revolution in Ukraine. Some of these revolutions have led to the overthrow of the government, while others have been less successful.

Vladimir Putin has been determined to prevent such occurrences in Russia. He blames Western influence for the political unrest, saying, "We see what tragic consequences the wave of so-called color revolutions led to. For us this is a lesson and a warning. We should do everything necessary so that nothing similar ever happens in Russia."[1] Such thinking has led Putin to use force and jail dissidents to crush Russian political protests when they have arisen in 2012 and 2017.

1. Quoted in Darya Korsunskaya, "Putin says Russia must Prevent 'Color Revolution,'" Reuters, November 20, 2014. www.reuters.com/article/us-russia-putin-security-idUSKCN0J41J620141120.

The Russian Federation

Gorbachev's successor, Boris Yeltsin, proved to be an ineffectual leader, unable to solve the countries' economic woes. Russia had lost its standing as a superpower. According to author John Green, the United States was left in something of a "policy limbo … The idea of a super-powerful, malevolent … Soviet Union poised to destroy the American way of life provided a comfortable structure for all our foreign relations for almost fifty years," as well as giving the United States a reason for building up its military "and all the jobs that came with it."[69]

With the Russian Federation suffering through growing pains and China not quite there yet, the United States was left as the world's only major superpower. Many Russians believe that the United States

> *sought to dictate to them, to marginalize and humiliate their country. America had flooded their country with its*

Boris Yeltsin, shown here, was the first President of the Russian Federation.

consumer goods, expanded NATO into Eastern Europe and the Baltic states ... acted with impunity in the Balkans, promoted color revolutions in the former Soviet republics, and piously lectured Russia on the inadequacies of its democratic experiment.[70]

Russian national pride had always been a driving force in the country's power and standing in the world. Now, Russia's self-image had hit rock bottom.

The Russian Federation was therefore primed for the ascension of another strong man who could possibly right all of these wrongs. His name was Vladimir Putin.

Putin's Rise

Despite the Russian Federation's self-description as a federal semi-presidential republic (meaning it has a president and a prime minister) with free elections and a multi-party

PUTIN CONFRONTS A MOB

Vladimir Putin's story goes back to 1989, when he was a Russian KGB spy in East Germany. The Soviet Union was breaking up, and the Berlin Wall had come down. Even a month later, German protesters were still roaming the streets of Dresden, Germany, ransacking government buildings. A mob arrived at the Russian KGB headquarters. Inside the building was a trove of secret Russian documents. The young Putin called Soviet military command asking for reinforcements. However, there was no response from the Soviet Government. "Moscow is silent," Putin was told. So Putin went to confront the mob, and he bluffed to them. "This house is strictly guarded," he said in perfect German. "My soldiers have weapons. And I gave them orders: if anyone enters the compound, they are to open fire."[1]

There were no such guards in the building, but Putin's ruse worked. The crowd dispersed. Still, Putin was scarred by the incident: "'I had the feeling then that the country [the Soviet Union] was no more,' he recalled, the bitterness still raw years later, 'that it had disappeared. It became clear the [Soviet] Union was ailing. It was a deadly, incurable disease called paralysis—a paralysis of power.'"[2]

1. Quoted in Steven Lee Myers, *The New Tsar: The Rise and Reign of Vladimir Putin*. New York, NY: Alfred A. Knopf, 2015, pp. 50–51.
2. Quoted in Myers, *The Rise and Reign of Vladimir Putin*, p. 50.

system, under Vladimir Putin, it has been forced back into a semblance of its former totalitarian self. Historian Stephen Kotkin describes Russia's current situation as "personal rule."[71] Biographer Steven Lee Myers titled his book on Putin, *The New Tsar*. Political scientist Karen Dawisha considers Putin's Russia to be a "kleptocracy" (a corrupt government). William Falk, editor-in-chief of *The Week*, minces no words, calling Putin "an amoral thug who loathes democracy and dissent, kills without conscience, and is aggressively conspiring to sow chaos in the Western world."[72]

Some of Gorbachev's reforms persist. For example, the country is no longer considered Communist, and personal freedoms also remain, if one does not use that freedom to criticize Putin's government. As Falk wrote, "It's dangerous to aggravate Vladimir Putin. You could slip and fall out a fourth-floor window, like Nikolai Gorokhov, a lawyer for a prominent Russian whistleblower. You could get assassinated on a Kiev street, like Denis Voronenkov, a Putin critic … You could get your country invaded, like the Ukrainians who in 2014 dared to overthrow the Putin puppet Viktor Yanukovych. You could get arrested and beaten for demonstrating against the rampant corruption … like tens of thousands of Russians did … You could even have Russian hackers try to disrupt your presidential election."[73]

Putin, former law student and spy, has built a career on trying to restore the old, lost Soviet power. He has described the collapse of the Soviet Union as "the major geopolitical disaster of the century."[74] Ever since, the Russian leader has fancied himself a defense against the chaos of the post-Soviet world. Though Presidents George W. Bush and Barack Obama both hoped to work with him early on, Putin maintained a deep distrust of the West, possibly as a result of his years as a spy for the Soviet security agency known as the KGB. The United States has found him to be a formidable opponent.

While serving in the KGB in Dresden, Germany, Putin watched as the Berlin Wall fell and the Soviet sphere of influence over Germany disintegrated. He was called back to Russia. In St. Petersburg (then still Leningrad), he served as deputy mayor under his former law professor, who had become mayor. In 1999, Boris Yeltsin appointed Putin prime minister. When the deeply unpopular and ineffectual Yeltsin resigned on December 31, 1999, Putin became interim president. After gaining popularity by crushing a rebellion in the Soviet state of Chechnya (and, in the process, killing tens of thousands of people), Putin was elected president in 2000. Despite his ruthlessness, he was viewed as a strong leader who could restore Russia to greatness.

According to Steven Kotkin, "Bit by bit … using stealth and dirty tricks, Putin reasserted central control over the levers of power within the country—the TV stations, the gas industry, the

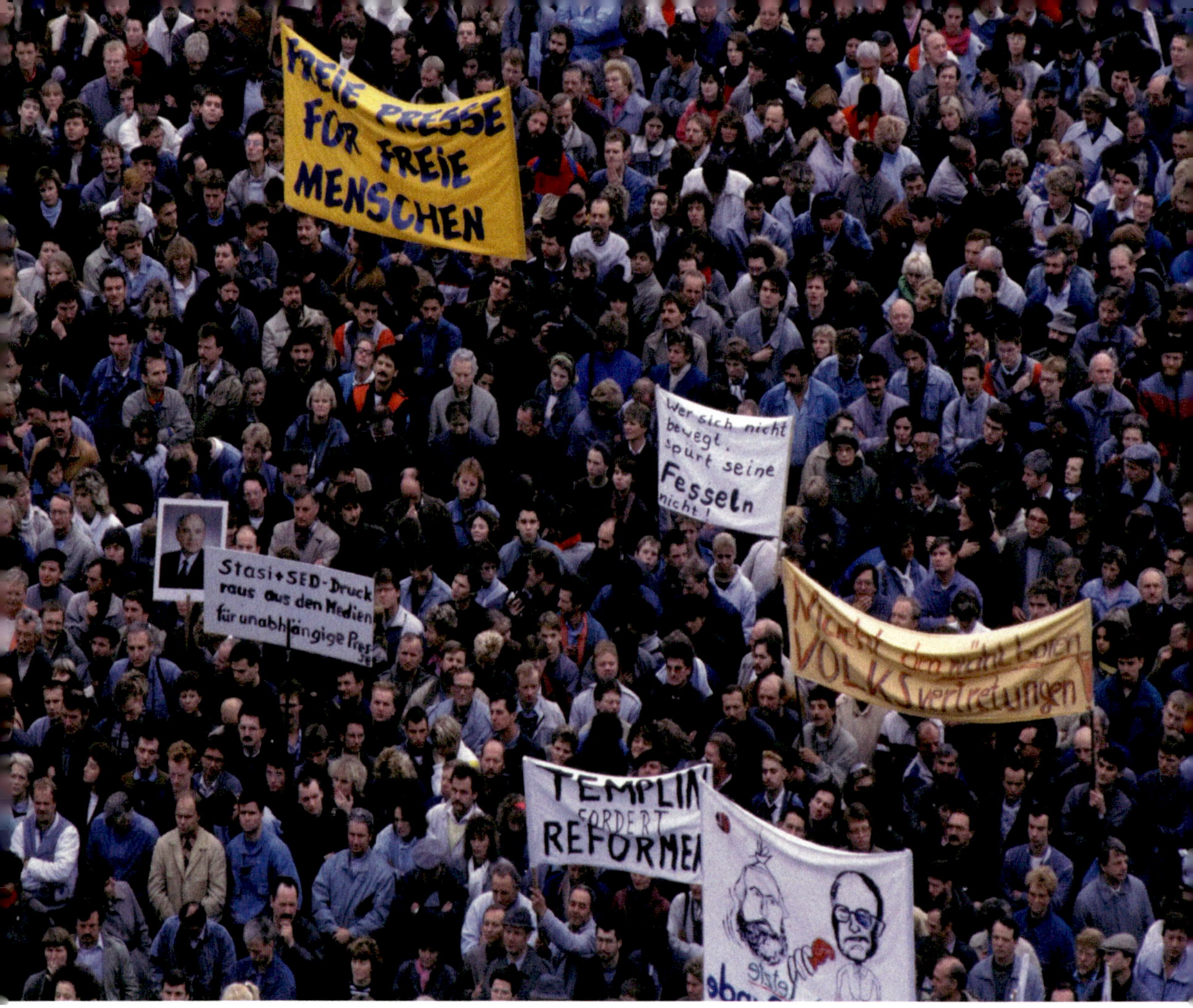

Germans are shown here demonstrating against the Communist regime in 1989.

oil industry, the regions."[75] Putin was aided by Russia's economy, which took off in 1999 and grew dramatically for a decade. The country's gross domestic product increased from $196 billion to approximately $2.1 trillion by 2013. It was reported that "Wages rose, pensions were doled out, and the immense national debt that had been accumulated by previous leaders was paid off early … Russia's stock market skyrocketed, increasing 20-fold."[76]

Because Russia's Constitution limited the president's tenure to two four-year terms, Putin stepped down in 2008 and installed Dmitry Medvedev as president, with Putin as a puppet-master prime minister. Four years later, Putin once again ran for president, and, in an election that many in both Russia and abroad considered fraudulent, was once more officially elevated to the chief role in the Russian Federation.

Putin versus the United States

The suspected corruption in the 2012 Russian election led to massive protests across Russia. Tens of thousands of Russians swarmed the streets of Moscow, accusing Putin's party, Russia United, of rigging the election, and demanding he step down. These were the largest protests in Russia in many years. Such chaos was Putin's greatest fear, as it was reminiscent of his days as a KGB operative when the Soviet Union collapsed. Fearing a color revolution of the sort that had occurred in various Russian satellites, Putin sent loyal paramilitary troops into the streets to crush the rebellion. He has essentially owned Russia ever since.

Many observers claim that Putin has used Russia as his personal piggy bank, getting rich thanks to noncompetitive privatization of state assets, no-bid government contracts, illegal loans, fake bankruptcies, tax "refunds," patriotic projects such as the Olympics, and other favors. His personal fortune has been estimated conservatively at $40 billion and generously at $200 billion. The latter figure would make him the richest man in the world.

Hillary Clinton was U.S. secretary of state when Putin reclaimed the presidency. President Barack Obama and Secretary Clinton had offered Russia a "reset" upon coming into office in 2008, and relations between the two countries had improved. (The Russian foreign minister disagrees with this characterization, claiming he got along fine with Clinton's predecessor, Condoleezza Rice.) Under Obama, Joby Warrick and Karen DeYoung wrote for the *Washington Post*, "The two governments had notched historic agreements, including a new treaty on reducing nuclear stockpiles and a pact allowing U.S. military planes to use Russian airspace in delivering supplies to troops [fighting the U.S. war] in Afghanistan."[77] Even so, Clinton had always been skeptical about working with Putin. In 2008, President George W. Bush famously stated that he had looked into Putin's eyes and gotten "a sense of his soul." Clinton later said, "He was a KGB agent—by definition he doesn't have a soul."[78]

The 2012 Russian election caused a new rift. In a speech, Secretary Clinton criticized Putin's coup. "The Russian people, like people everywhere, deserve the right to have their voices heard and their votes counted," she said. "And that means they deserve fair, free, transparent elections and leaders who are accountable to them."[79]

When the demonstrations in Moscow grew larger after Clinton's speech, the Russian leader blamed Clinton for inciting his people against him. "Putin … [said that] Clinton gave 'a signal' to demonstrators working 'with the support of the U.S. State Department' to undermine his power. 'We need to safeguard ourselves from this interference in our internal affairs,' Putin declared."[80] Russian expert Clifford Kupchan summed up the situation: "Putin has kind of got it in for Hillary … The statements [she made during the protests] were like kerosene on a fire, and it really made Putin angry."[81]

The public had largely forgotten Clinton's words by the time she ran for president in 2016, but not Putin. "This history is real," said U.S. ambassador to Moscow Michael McFaul, "and Putin doesn't forget these things."[82] With Putin firmly in power in 2016, retribution was perhaps inevitable. "He was very

Hillary Clinton and Russian leader Vladimir Putin are shown here.

upset [with Clinton] and continued to be for the rest of the time that I was in government," said Michael McFaul, former U.S. ambassador to Moscow. "One could speculate that [the 2016 U.S. election] is his moment for payback."[83]

In 2017, Sam Ellis observed, "Putin's power has come at enormous cost—Russia's population is shrinking, its life expectancy is falling, and its economy is in the midst of a prolonged recession—but ordinary Russians don't seem to care. Seventeen years after Putin became Russia's president, there's no sign of if, or when, the Putin era will come to a close."[84]

EPILOGUE

RUSSIA IN THE 21ST CENTURY

The story of Russia in the 21st century is the story of Vladimir Putin, who rules with an iron fist. As Stanislav Belkovsky said, "The search for Russia's national idea, which began after the dissolution of the Soviet Union, is finally over. Now it is evident that Russia's national idea is Vladimir Vladimirovich Putin."[85] "His loyal friends," according to Gal Beckerman, "now run most of Russia's important industries." His advisors call his leadership style "'managed democracy,' providing only the semblance of popular will." He has stated that "The Russian people are backward. They cannot adapt to democracy as they have done in [other] countries. They need time."[86]

As a former Soviet spy, Putin does not trust the West. Therefore, like Stalin before him, his plans extend beyond Russia. He wants to put a buffer in between his country and Europe, and he wants to control as much of the world as he can. A weak NATO would facilitate such matters—so would a weakened United States. Such plans, combined with Putin's hatred of Hillary Rodham Clinton, played out on the world stage in 2016.

Putin and Trump

During Donald Trump's campaign for president of the United States, the optics—meaning the way things looked—seemed suspicious to some. Trump seemingly surrounded himself with campaign chairmen, advisors, confidantes, and friends who had strong ties to Russia. Trump's second campaign manager, Paul Manafort, was forced to step down over his Russian connections. Manafort, a veteran lobbyist and political consultant, had worked for Vladimir Putin's ally in Ukraine, former president Viktor Yanukovych, from 2006 to 2012. Yanukovych was driven from office after Ukrainians staged protests about his close ties to Moscow. Revelations in the summer of 2016 that Manafort might have accepted $12.7 million dollars in illegal payments from Yanukovych's government forced his resignation from the Trump campaign.

Trump's former campaign director, Paul Manafort (shown here), was indicted in October 2017 on charges of conspiracy and money laundering. He surrendered to the FBI but pled not guilty.

Trump's pick for National Security Advisor, former U.S. General Michael Flynn, also stepped down after it was learned that he had potentially inappropriate conversations with the Russian ambassador to the United States, Sergey Kislyak, and subsequently lied about them to Vice President-elect Mike Pence. Jared Kushner, Trump's son-in-law, also met with Kislyak in Trump Tower during this time and reportedly attempted to develop a "back channel," a secret and secure communications pathway between the Trump transition team and the Kremlin—the center of the Russian government. Trump foreign policy advisor, Carter Page, according to U.S. intelligence, was once targeted by a Russian spy as a possible source of information and passed documents about the U.S. energy industry to the Russians. President Trump's son, Donald Trump Jr., along with Manafort and Kushner, met with a Russian attorney who had

Michael Flynn, shown here, stepped down after having conversations with Sergey Kislyak.

promised them damaging information on Hillary Clinton.

Secretary of State Rex Tillerson, Attorney General Jefferson Sessions, Secretary of Commerce Wilbur Ross, advisor Roger Stone, and Trump business associate Felix Sater all have close ties to the Russian Federation. Despite Donald Trump's denials that he had anything to do with Russia and that he did little to no business there, Donald Trump Jr. was quoted in 2008 as saying, "Russians make up a pretty disproportionate cross-section of a lot of our [business] assets."[87]

Trump raised many eyebrows in the United States over his positive comments about Putin. "Throughout the 2016 presidential campaign, Donald Trump consistently broke from political orthodoxy in his effusive praise of Russian President Vladimir Putin,"[88] CNN reporters Andrew Kaczynski, Chris Massie, and Nathan McDermott wrote. Trump has often praised Putin's leadership, contrasting the Russian's strength with the supposed weakness of Trump's predecessor, Barack Obama. When journalist George Stephanopoulos raised the subject of Putin's alleged murders of journalists, Trump responded, "I think it would be despicable if that took place, but I haven't seen any evidence that he killed anybody in terms of reporters."[89] When Trump ally Bill O'Reilly of Fox News called Putin a killer, Trump responded, "There are a lot of killers. You think our country's so innocent?"[90] Putin, for his part, has returned Trump's praise. "He's a really brilliant and talented person, without any doubt,"[91] Putin said of Trump in December 2015. Upon Trump's election in 2016, Putin told reporters, "Because he achieved success in business, it suggests that he is a clever man. And if (he is) a clever man, then he will fully and quite quickly understand another level of responsibility. We assume that he will be acting from these positions."[92]

According to CNN, "Since 2013—when Trump's Miss Universe pageant was held in Moscow—Trump has at least nine times claimed to have spoken to, met, or made contact with Putin."[93] In 2013, while in Moscow for the Miss Universe Pageant, Trump said, "I do have a relationship [with Putin] and I can tell you he's very interested in what we're doing here today."[94] However, during Trump's campaign, once the media picked up on potential Russian ties, Trump's statements about Putin changed, and he began to deny ever meeting with Putin or even knowing who the Russian leader was. "I never met Putin," Trump said in July 2016. "I don't know who Putin is. He said one nice thing about me. He said I'm a genius. I said thank you very much to the newspaper and that was the end of it. I never met Putin."[95]

Russia and the 2016 U.S. Election

According to U.S. intelligence, Vladimir Putin was more involved in the 2016 U.S. presidential election than many

U.S. citizens. Michael Morell, former acting director of the CIA, called Russia's interference in the 2016 U.S. election "the political equivalent of [the] 9/11 [terrorist attacks]" and "an attack on our very democracy."[96] In October 2016, then Director of National Intelligence, Jim Clapper, put out a statement that the Russians were attempting to interfere in the U.S. elections. According to Morell, the hacking was done "at the direction of Vladimir Putin."[97]

Morell claimed the Russians had a specific aim in mind: to undermine the candidacy of Secretary Hillary Clinton and to promote the election of Donald J. Trump. Morell further stated that the Russians attempted to "hack" the election in three specific ways: First, by stealing Hillary Clinton's campaign director John Podesta's emails and providing them to the website Wikileaks; second, by disseminating fake news and damaging stories about Hillary Clinton on social media; and finally, by directly attempting to hack into voting machines. Morell said that while the first two methods were successful, hacking the actual machines was much more difficult than the Russians believed and could not be accomplished.

Wikileaks founder, Julian Assange (shown here), published documents from Hillary Clinton campaign manager John Podesta.

Russia got an assist from Wikileaks founder Julian Assange, who also had strong reasons to detest Clinton and Obama. In 2010, a U.S. intelligence analyst now known as Chelsea Manning leaked vast amounts of classified documents that were subsequently published on Wikileaks. Manning was court-martialed and spent years in prison until Obama commuted the sentence in 2017.

At the time of the leaks, Hillary Clinton, as secretary of state, was forceful in her condemnation of Assange, saying that his release of classified U.S. documents "puts people's lives in danger, threatens our national security and undermines our efforts to work with other countries to solve shared problems."[98] Assange believed that Clinton was among those in the United States who had tried to bring criminal charges against him for posting the classified documents.

Fast forward six years, and Assange had his revenge. "WikiLeaks' dump of nearly 20,000 hacked emails taken from the Democratic National Committee was timed to do maximum damage to Hillary Clinton's presidential campaign,"[99] journalist Jacob Siegel wrote. At the time, Assange strongly denied that he received the leaked emails from Russian contacts, but American intelligence has since determined that Russia was undoubtedly behind the hacks.

Much speculation continues to surround the role Russian interference played in the results of the 2016 presidential election, in which Donald Trump defeated Hillary Clinton. American intelligence was surprised with the

Donald Trump and Hillary Clinton are shown here debating during the presidential campaign of 2016.

ease with which they traced the hacking back to Russian sources. Russian journalist Yevgenia Albats had an answer for this—Putin was not concerned with running a secret operation. Putin probably did not believe that he could affect the results in the U.S. election, Albats explained, but "'[h]e wanted to make it as public as possible. He wanted his presence to be known,' and to 'show that, no matter what, we [Russia] can enter your house and do what we want.'"[100]

Once it became clear that the meddling had occurred, Barack Obama levied sanctions on the Russian government. He ordered 35 Russian officials booted out of the United States and closed 2 diplomatic compounds.

The United States expected Putin to retaliate, but no reprisal occurred. U.S. intelligence knows that former Trump National Security Advisor Michael Flynn had conversations with Russia's U.S. ambassador, Sergey Kislyak, around this time. Speculation abounds that Flynn promised the Russians that Obama's sanctions would be lifted once Trump took office.

Trump continued to deny that the Russians interfered in the election, suggesting that the accusations were excuses on the part of the defeated Democrats. He used his Twitter account to deny the story and call for an end to the investigation into the claims of Russian involvement in the election. As the FBI dug deeper into Trump's Russian connections, Trump abruptly fired FBI Director James Comey. However, an investigation into ties between Trump associates and Russia continued under the direction of Robert Mueller.

For his part, Vladimir Putin continued to vehemently deny any state-sponsored Russian meddling in the U.S. election. However, in June 2017, he made a startling admission that private, "patriotically minded" Russian hackers, offended by the Obama administration's (and Hillary Clinton's) attitude toward their country, might have launched the cyberattacks against U.S. targets.

Trump as President

Questions about Russia continued to dog Donald Trump even after his inauguration in January 2017. Meanwhile, in Russia, government officials and official press greeted Trump's inauguration with unbridled happiness. The Obama-Clinton American liberal wing had been dealt a crushing defeat, they believed, and they believed a new order was about to emerge, one that would not stand in the way of Putin's ambitions. One Russian paper went so far as to compare the Trump victory to that of the Bolsheviks in 1917:

> *"In 1917, armed supporters of Lenin stormed the Winter Palace and arrested capitalist ministers and overthrew the social political order," the lead article in the daily* Moskovski Komsomolets *read. "On January 20, 2017, nobody in Washington planned*

THE COMPLEX CONFLICT IN SYRIA

As a proxy war involving the United States, Russia, Iran, and many of the Middle Eastern countries, the Syrian conflict is complicated. The civil war began with Arab Spring protests in 2011, after Syrian dictator Bashar al-Assad's soldiers opened fire on demonstrators. A rebel force formed in reaction to this aggression, and the two sides have been battling ever since. The rebels have received support from the United States, Saudi Arabia, and other Middle Eastern countries. Assad's allies include Iran, Russia, and the terrorist group Hezbollah.

The war has been brutal, as Assad has on occasion dropped chemical weapons on his foes as well as on civilians. Such brutality has caused the Syrian refugee crisis, with innocent families fleeing to Europe by the millions. Anti-immigration politics in Europe and the United States has arisen as a result of the fear that such massive numbers of refugees might be hiding isolated terrorists.

In 2014, the Islamic State in Iraq and Syria (ISIS) entered the fray, seizing swathes of northern Syria to establish its caliphate. Despite being backed by Russia and Iran, Assad had been losing great portions of the country. Therefore, in 2015, Russia stepped in, supposedly to bomb ISIS, but in reality bombing the Syrian rebels, including those backed by the United States.

It is clear that the civil war in Syria will have serious ramifications for the rest of the world for years to come.

to storm Congress or the White House … but the feeling of the American political élite, especially the liberal part of it, is not different from that of the Russian bourgeoisie one hundred years ago.[101]

However, Donald Trump's presidency did not usher in the peace and prosperity for which the Russians were hoping. Due to the rampant suspicions about Russian interference in the 2016 election that dominated the American news in 2017, Trump has not had the political capital to lift the Russian sanctions. Tensions continue to be high over Russia's annexation of Ukraine and its threat to the rest of Eastern Europe, over North Korea (which shares a border with southeastern Russia), and over Syria.

The ongoing civil war in Syria between President Bashar al-Assad and Syrian rebels reached a boiling point on April 4, 2017, when Syrian civilians, including women and children, were killed by sarin gas. The deployment of chemical weapons has been a war crime since the Geneva Protocol of 1975. Russia has supported the Assad regime, while the United States has backed the rebels. Barack Obama had threatened direct military action in 2013 after a similar chemical attack, but backed away, as the United States was already war weary from its conflicts in Afghanistan and Iraq. Russia promised to force Assad to give up his chemical weaponry at that time, but he did not do so. The conflict rages on, and on April 6, 2017, President Trump sent 59 Tomahawk cruise missiles to destroy much of the airbase from which the Syrians had launched the chemical attacks. This strike angered the Russians, who in public statements, claimed that they were not entirely convinced that Assad used poison gas. Vladimir Putin called the U.S. attack a violation of international law and a blow to U.S.-Russian relations. Prime Minister Medvedev said the attack ruined the two countries' rapport. In an address following the Syrian bombing, Donald Trump stated, "We're not getting along with Russia at all. We may be at an all-time low."[102] However, some people questioned if relations were truly at a historically low point or if Trump was perhaps overstating for emphasis.

Europe also continues to be on high alert, as Putin's aggressive expansion into the Ukraine in 2014 has left countries bordering Russia fearful that Putin may act again. Estonia, Latvia, and Lithuania, Russia's three Baltic neighbors, have increased their military spending dramatically in the past few years. "If you're in Estonia, or Latvia, and Russia's sitting there on your border, it's scary,"[103] said Jill Russell of the Defense Studies Department at King's College London. Consequently, NATO forces were deployed to Estonia, Latvia, Lithuania, and Poland in early 2017. "NATO's risk assessment shows 'there is currently a threat to the bloc from our eastern neighbor,' [Estonian President Kersti] Kaljulaid said. 'That's why the NATO battalion is needed here and why there have to be contingency plans for protecting the alliance.'"[104]

On the campaign trail in 2016, Trump often spoke against NATO, calling it useless in the current world, questioning America's financial commitment to it, and calling upon other countries to pay more money to support the organization. Such comments have played right into Putin's hands, as it is clear that he would like nothing more than a weakened NATO. However, in mid-April 2017, Trump reversed his position, claiming that NATO was no longer obsolete.

Russia's supposed interference in elections in England, Germany, and France has strengthened suspicions in the West against Putin. "On a regular basis they try to influence elections in Europe,"[105] Barack Obama stated. As with Russian interference in the United States, Putin supports nationalist movements in European countries that will focus on the country's domestic issues while ignoring international ones. Such

The USS Porter *launched Tomahawk missiles toward the al-Shayrat airbase in Syria in response to chemical attacks on Syrian civilians.*

priorities would give Putin free reign in Eastern Europe. However, Putin's master plan stalled in France, where, in May 2017, the centrist, Emmanuel Macron, won a solid victory in the presidential election over the hard right candidate favored by the Russian leader, Marine Le Pen.

In July 2017, Putin and Trump sat face-to-face for the first time as leaders of their nations, and Trump reportedly pressed the Russian leader about meddling in the 2016 election. Putin denied everything. "Our position is well-known," Putin later told reporters regarding his conversation with Trump. "There is no ground to believe that Russia interfered in the U.S. electoral process."[106] While Putin claimed that Trump was satisfied with this answer, Trump's people subsequently put out conflicting statements about whether or not he accepted Putin's assurances. President Trump stated that it was time to relegate the Russian story to the past and to move forward, and perhaps even to work jointly with the Russians on cybersecurity. However, United Nations ambassador Nikki Haley, a Trump appointee, said Putin "did exactly what we thought he would do, which is deny" Russian involvement in the U.S. election. Haley added, "we can't trust Russia and we won't ever trust Russia."[107]

In a famous speech of 1966, during the height of the Cold War, John F. Kennedy's younger brother, Robert Kennedy, told listeners that it was not their lot in life to live in a comfortable era. He declared, "There is a ... curse which says 'May he live in interesting times.' Like it or not, we live in interesting times."[108] Even though the Cold War is over, Kennedy's words still ring true today.

Notes

Introduction:
Iconic Moments in Russian-American Relations

1. Gerald M. Boyd, "Raze Berlin Wall, Reagan Urges Soviet," *New York Times*, June 13, 1987. www.nytimes.com/1987/06/13/world/raze-berlin-wall-reagan-urges-soviet.html.
2. Romesh Ratnesar, "20 Years After 'Tear Down this Wall,'" *TIME*, June 11, 2007. content.time.com/time/world/article/0,8599,1631828,00.html.
3. Mikhail Gorbachev, "End of the Soviet Union; Text of Gorbachev's Farewell Address," *New York Times*, December 26, 1991. www.nytimes.com/1991/12/26/world/end-of-the-soviet-union-text-of-gorbachev-s-farewell-address.html?pagewanted=all.

Chapter One:
Early Russian and American Relations

4. Charles E. Ziegler, "Russian-American Relations: From Tsarism to Putin," *International Politics*, Vol. 51, 6, p. 672.
5. John Lewis Gaddis, *Russia, The Soviet Union, and the United States: An Interpretive History*. New York, NY: Knopf, 1978, p. 1.
6. Norman E. Saul, *Distant Friends: The United States and Russia 1763-1867*. Lawrence, KS: University Press of Kansas, 1991, p. 3.
7. Saul, *Distant Friends*, p. 3.
8. Saul, *Distant Friends*, p. 3.
9. Nikolai V. Sivachev and Nikolai N. Yakovlev, *Russia and the United States: U.S.-Soviet Relations from the Soviet Point of View*. Chicago, IL: University of Chicago Press, 1979, p. 1.
10. Frank A. Golder, "Catherine II and the American Revolution," *American Historical Review*, Vol. 21, No. 1 (1915), p. 92.
11. Golder, "Catherine II and the American Revolution," p. 93.
12. Golder, "Catherine II and the American Revolution," p. 95.

13. Quoted in Nikolai N. Bolkhovitinov, *The Beginnings of Russian-American Relations 1775-1815*. Cambridge, MA: Harvard University Press, 1975, p. 10.

14. Bolkhovitinov, *The Beginnings of Russian-American Relations 1775-1815*, p. 10.

15. Golder, "Catherine II and the American Revolution," p. 95.

16. Saul, *Distant Friends*, p. 15.

17. Saul, *Distant Friends*, p. 15.

18. Saul, *Distant Friends*, p. 11.

19. Bolkhovitinov, *The Beginnings of Russian-American Relations 1775-1815*, p. 10.

Chapter Two: World War I, the Russian Revolution, and the Aftermath

20. Christopher Klein, "The Russian Revolution, Through American Eyes," History.com. March 8, 2017. www.history.com/news/the-russian-revolution-through-american-eyes.

21. Richard Pipes, *A Concise History of the Russian Revolution*. New York, NY: Vintage, 1995, pp. 96–97.

22. Pipes, *A Concise History of the Russian Revolution*, p. 97.

23. Pipes, *A Concise History of the Russian Revolution*, p. 226.

24. Pipes, *A Concise History of the Russian Revolution*, pp. 227–228.

25. Thomas A. Bailey, *America Faces Russia: Russian-American Relations From Early Times to Our Day*. Ithaca, NY: Cornell University Press, 1950, p. 239.

26. Quoted in Barry Rubin and Judith Colp Rubin, *Hating America: A History*. Oxford, UK: Oxford University Press, 2004, p. 80.

27. Carl J. Richard, *When the United States Invaded Russia: Woodrow Wilson's Siberian Disaster*. Lanham, MD: Rowman and Littlefield, 2013, p. 169.

28. Bailey, *America Faces Russia: Russian-American Relations From Early Times to Our Day*, p. 248.

29. Peter G. Boyle, *American-Soviet Relations: From the Russian Revolution to the Fall of Communism*. New York, NY: Rutledge, 1993, pp. 13–14.

30. Boyle, *American-Soviet Relations*, p. 21.

31. Katherine A.S. Siegel, *Loans and Legitimacy: The Evolution of Soviet-American Relations 1919–1933*. Lexington, KY: The University of Kentucky Press, 1996, pp. 1–2.

Chapter Three: World War II

32. Quoted in Josh Zeitz, "The Speech That Set Off the Debate About America's Role in the World," *Politico*, December 29, 2015. www.politico.com/magazine/story/2015/12/roosevelt-arsenal-of-democracy-speech-213483.
33. Bailey, *America Faces Russia: Russian-American Relations From Early Times to Our Day*, p. 289.
34. Mark Steinberg, *A History of Russia: From Peter the Great to Gorbachev*. The Great Courses, 2003. www.thegreatcourses.com/courses/history-of-russia-from-peter-the-great-to-gorbachev.html.
35. Quoted in Stephen E. Ambrose, *Rise to Globalism: American Foreign Policy Since 1938*, 4th ed. New York, NY: Penguin, 1985, p. 58.
36. Thomas A. Bailey, *A Diplomatic History of the American People*. New York, NY: Appleton-Century-Crofts, 1958, p. 778.
37. Gar Alperovitz, *The Decision to Use the Atomic Bomb and The Architecture of an American Myth*. New York, NY: Alfred A. Knopf, 1995, p. 239.

Chapter Four: The Cold War

38. Winston Churchill, "The Sinews of Peace ('Iron Curtain Speech')," The International Churchill Society, March 5, 1946. www.winstonchurchill.org/resources/speeches/1946-1963-elder-statesman/120-the-sinews-of-peace.
39. Churchill, "The Sinews of Peace ('Iron Curtain Speech')."
40. Quoted in Sivachev and Yakovlev, *Russia and the United States: U.S.-Soviet Relations from the Soviet Point of View*, p. 219.
41. Sivachev and Yakovlev, *Russia and the United States: U.S.-Soviet Relations from the Soviet Point of View*, p. 219.
42. George F. Kennan, "The Sources of Soviet Conduct (1947)," America: A Narrative History, accessed August 30, 2017. www.wwnorton.com/college/history/america7/content/multimedia/ch31/documents_02.htm.
43. Boyle, *American-Soviet Relations*, p. 255.
44. Harry S. Truman, "President Harry S. Truman's Address Before a Joint Session of Congress, March 12, 1947," The Avalon Project, March 12, 1947. avalon.law.yale.edu/20th_century/trudoc.asp.

45. George C. Marshall, "The Marshall Plan Speech," The George C. Marshall Foundation, accessed August 31, 2017. marshallfoundation.org/marshall/the-marshall-plan/marshall-plan-speech/.

46. "Cold War—Chapter 2: 'Containment,'" YouTube video, 13:12, posted by Media Rich Learning on March 5, 2015. www.youtube.com/watch?v=7vdXLkWUjrU.

47. Bailey, *A Diplomatic History of the American People*, p. 809.

48. William Faulkner, "William Faulkner—Banquet Speech," NobelPrize.org, December 10, 1950. www.nobelprize.org/nobel_prizes/literature/laureates/1949/faulkner-speech.html.

49. Alperovitz, *The Decision to Use the Atomic Bomb and The Architecture of an American Myth*, p. 355.

50. Alperovitz, *The Decision to Use the Atomic Bomb and The Architecture of an American Myth*, p. 127.

51. Quoted in Alperovitz, *The Decision to Use the Atomic Bomb and The Architecture of an American Myth*, p. 127.

52. Quoted in Alperovitz, *The Decision to Use the Atomic Bomb and The Architecture of an American Myth*, p. 128.

53. U.S. Department of Energy, The Manhattan Project: An Interactive History, accessed September 3, 2017. www.osti.gov/opennet/manhattan-project-history/Events/1942-1945/espionage.htm.

54. Quoted in History.com Staff, "McCarthy says Communists are in State Department." History.com, 2009. www.history.com/this-day-in-history/mccarthy-says-communists-are-in-state-department.

55. "McCarthy-Welch Exchange," American Rhetoric, accessed September 3, 2017. www.americanrhetoric.com/speeches/welch-mccarthy.html.

56. Boyle, *American-Soviet Relations*, p. 138.

57. Sivachev and Yakovlev, *Russia and the United States: U.S.-Soviet Relations from the Soviet Point of View*, p. 244.

58. Ho Chi Minh, "Ho's Appeal at the Founding of the Communist Party of Indochina, 1930," in Robert J. McMahon, ed. *Major Problems in the History of the Vietnam War*. Lexington, MA: D.C. Heath and Company, 1990, p. 34.

59. Dwight D. Eisenhower, President Eisenhower's News Conference, April 7, 1954, *Public Papers of the Presidents*, accessed September 3, 2017. www.mtholyoke.edu/acad/intrel/pentagon/ps11.htm.

60. Ho Chi Minh, "Letter from Ho Chi Minh to President Lyndon Johnson," Digital History, accessed September 3, 2017. www.digitalhistory.uh.edu/disp_textbook.cfm?smtID=3&psid=3641.

61. Daniel S. Papp, *Contemporary International Relations: Frameworks for Understanding*. New York, NY: MacMillan, 1984, p. 136.

62. "USSR 'Secret' Vietnam Soldiers Speak Out," YouTube video, 2:18, posted by RT on February 16, 2008. www.youtube.com/watch?v=6wprT66Yjxs.

63. Papp, *Contemporary International Relations: Frameworks for Understanding*, p. 137.

64. "Half-way from Rags to Riches," *The Economist*, April 24, 2008. www.economist.com/node/11041638.

Chapter Five:
The End of the Cold War and the Rise of Vladimir Putin

65. Boyle, *American-Soviet Relations*, p. 213.

66. Sam Ellis, "From Spy to President: The Rise of Vladimir Putin." *Vox*. March 27, 2017. www.vox.com/videos/2017/3/27/15052666/putin-russia-spy-president-vladimir.

67. Gorbachev, "End of the Soviet Union; Text of Gorbachev's Farewell Address."

68. Gorbachev, "End of the Soviet Union; Text of Gorbachev's Farewell Address."

69. "George HW Bush and the End of the Cold War: Crash Course US History #44," YouTube video, 13:52, posted by CrashCourse on January 16, 2014. www.youtube.com/watch?v=L-K19rVDxoM.

70. Charles E. Ziegler, *The History of Russia*. 2nd Ed. Santa Barbara, CA: Greenwood, 2009, p. 201.

71. Stephen Kotkin, "The Resistible Rise of Vladimir Putin," *Foreign Affairs*, March/April 2015. www.foreignaffairs.com/reviews/resistible-rise-vladimir-putin.

72. William Falk, "Editor's Letter," *The Week*, April 7, 2017. theweek.com/articles/689316/no-more-illusions-about-putin.

73. Falk, "Editor's Letter."

74. Quoted in Ellis, "From Spy to President: The Rise of Vladimir Putin."

75. Kotkin, "The Resistible Rise of Vladimir Putin."

76. Kotkin, "The Resistible Rise of Vladimir Putin."

77. Joby Warrick and Karen DeYoung, "From "Reset to "Pause': The Real Story Behind Hillary Clinton's Feud with Vladimir Putin," *Washington Post*, November 3, 2016. www.washingtonpost.com/world/national-security/from-reset-to-pause-the-real-story-behind-hillary-clintons-feud-with-vladimir-putin/2016/11/03/f575f9fa-a116-11e6-8832-23a007c77bb4_story.html?utm_term=.d521b5347b46.

78. Warrick and DeYoung, "From "Reset to "Pause': The Real Story Behind Hillary Clinton's Feud with Vladimir Putin."

79. Warrick and DeYoung, "From "Reset to "Pause': The Real Story Behind Hillary Clinton's Feud with Vladimir Putin."

80. Michael Crowley and Julia Ioffe, "Why Putin Hates Hillary,"*Politico*, July 25, 2016. www.politico.com/story/2016/07/clinton-putin-226153.

81. Warrick and DeYoung, "From "Reset to "Pause': The Real Story Behind Hillary Clinton's Feud with Vladimir Putin."

82. Warrick and DeYoung, "From "Reset to "Pause': The Real Story Behind Hillary Clinton's Feud with Vladimir Putin."

83. Crowley and Ioffe, "Why Putin Hates Hillary."

84. Ellis, "From Spy to President: The Rise of Vladimir Putin."

Epilogue: Russia in the 21st Century

85. Quoted in Kotkin, "The Resistible Rise of Vladimir Putin."

86 Quoted in Gal Beckerman, "'The New Tsar: The Rise and Reign of Vladimir Putin,' by Steven Lee Myers," *New York Times*, November 2, 2015. www.nytimes.com/2015/11/08/books/review/the-new-tsar-the-rise-and-reign-of-vladimir-putin-by-steven-lee-myers.html?_r=0.

87. Evan Osnos, David Remnick, and Joshua Yaffa, "Trump, Putin, and the New Cold War," *The New Yorker*, March 6, 2017. www.newyorker.com/magazine/2017/03/06/trump-putin-and-the-new-cold-war.

88. Andrew Kaczynski, Chris Massie, and Nathan McDermott, "80 Times Trump Talked about Putin," CNN, accessed September 3, 2017. www.cnn.com/interactive/2017/03/politics/trump-putin-russia-timeline/.

89. Gideon Resnick, "Trump on Putin: Take His Word For It," *The Daily Beast*, December 20, 2015. www.thedailybeast.com/articles/2015/12/20/trump-on-putin-take-his-word-for-it.html.

90. Sophie Tatum, "Trump Defends Putin: 'You Think our Country's so Innocent?,'" CNN, February 6, 2017. www.cnn.com/2017/02/04/politics/donald-trump-vladimir-putin/.

91. Ann Marie Awad, "Vladimir Putin calls Donald Trump 'Brilliant and Talented Person,'" *UPI*, December 17, 2015. www.upi.com/Top_News/US/2015/12/17/Vladimir-Putin-calls-Donald-Trump-brilliant-and-talented-person/4331450359311/.

92. "Putin says Trump Clever, will Understand new Responsibilities," Reuters, December 4, 2016. www.reuters.com/article/us-usa-trump-putin-idUSKBN13T0B7.

93. Kaczynski, Massie, and McDermott,"80 Times Trump Talked about Putin."

94. Philip Bump, "Does Trump Know Putin? A Chronology," *Washington Post*, February 7, 2017. www.washingtonpost.com/news/politics/wp/2017/02/07/does-trump-know-putin-a-chronology/?utm_term=.db486b9a247c.

95. Kaczynski, Massie, and McDermott,"80 Times Trump Talked about Putin."

96. Charlie Rose, "Interview with Michael Morell," *The Charlie Rose Show*, December 14, 2016. charlierose.com/videos/29625.

97. Charlie Rose, "Interview with Michael Morell," *The Charlie Rose Show*, March 23, 2017. charlierose.com/videos/30288.

98. CNN Wire Staff, "Clinton Condemns Leak as 'Attack on International Community,'" CNN, November 30, 2010. www.cnn.com/2010/US/11/29/wikileaks/.

99. Jacob Siegel, "The Origin of Julian Assange's War on Hillary Clinton," *The Daily Beast*, September 17, 2016. www.thedailybeast.com/articles/2016/09/07/the-origin-of-julian-assange-and-wikileaks-war-on-hillary-clinton.html.

100. Osnos, Remnick, and Yaffa, "Trump, Putin, and the New Cold War."

101. Quoted in Osnos, Remnick, and Yaffa, "Trump, Putin, and the New Cold War."

102. Julian Borger and Alec Luhn, "Donald Trump says US Relations with Russia 'May Be at All-time Low.'" *The Guardian*. April 13, 2017. www.theguardian.com/us-news/2017/apr/12/us-russia-relations-tillerson-moscow-press-conference.

103. Quoted in Nolan Peterson, "Europe Quietly Arms Itself Against a Russian Invasion," *Newsweek*, November 6, 2016. www.newsweek.com/europe-quietly-arms-itself-against-russian-invasion-516634.

104. Quoted in Ott Ummelas, "NATO's Build-Up in East Cuts Fear of Conflict, Estonia Says," *Bloomberg Politics*, April 9, 2017. www.bloomberg.com/politics/articles/2017-04-09/eastern-nato-reinforcement-cuts-fear-of-conflict-estonia-says.

105. Quoted in Massimo Calebresi, "Hacking the Voter," *TIME*, October 10, 2016, p. 30.

106. Morgan Winsor, "Putin Claims Trump is 'Satisfied' with his Answers on Alleged Election Meddling," ABC News, July 8, 2017. abcnews.go.com/Politics/putin-claims-trump-satisfied-answers-alleged-election-meddling/story?id=48520913.

107. "'We Cannot Trust Russia and We Won't Ever Trust Russia'—US envoy to UN," *RT*. July 9, 2017. www.rt.com/usa/395814-us-trust-russia-haley/.

108. Robert Kennedy, "Day of Affirmation Address, University of Capetown, Capetown, South Africa, June 6, 1966," John F. Kennedy Presidential Library and Museum, accessed September 3, 2017. www.jfklibrary.org/Research/Research-Aids/Ready-Reference/RFK-Speeches/Day-of-Affirmation-Address-as-delivered.aspx.

For More Information

Books:

Dawisha, Karen. *Putin's Kleptocracy: Who owns Russia?* New York, NY: Simon and Schuster, 2015.
This book is a fascinating look at the man who has come to rule Russia and what his dominance means for the Russians and for the world.

Hosking, Geoffrey A. *Russian History: A Very Short Introduction*. Oxford, UK: Oxford University Press, 2012.
Hosking's book is a quick guide to the history of Russia from earliest times to the 21st century.

McMeekin, Sean. *The Russian Revolution*. New York, NY: Basic Books, 2017.
McMeekin examines the events that made up the period from the Russian Revolution to the rise of Communism.

Reed, John. *Ten Days That Shook the World*. New York, NY: Penguin, 2017.
This book is a description of the Russian Revolution from an American observer.

Wested, Odd Arne. *The Cold War: A World History*. New York, NY: Hachette, 2017.
This book provides plenty of thorough information on the entirety of the Cold War.

Websites:

Brookings Institution
(www.brookings.edu/topic/u-s-foreign-policy/)
The Brookings Institution is a general U.S. foreign policy website containing numerous articles on Russia from the Washington, D.C. think tank.

Embassy of the Russian Federation
(www.russianembassy.org/page/russian-american-relations)
The embassy website discusses U.S.-Russian relations from the Russian Federation's point of view and includes current events and press releases.

***Foreign Policy* Magazine**
(foreignpolicy.com/)
This website for the print magazine has numerous current articles on U.S. international relations, including those with Russia.

The *Huffington Post*: US Russia Relations
(www.huffingtonpost.com/news/us-russia-relations/)
This section of the *Huffington Post* contains a wide variety of up-to-date articles about U.S.-Russia relations.

The Library of Congress: Revelations from the Russian Archives
(www.loc.gov/exhibits/archives/sovi.html)
This website has an archive of original documents from the history of Russian-American relations.

Index

Picture Credits

Cover (top), p. 63 Sovfoto/UIG via Getty Images; cover (bottom-left) Mikhail Metzel\TASS via Getty Images; cover (bottom-middle) Basri Sahin/Anadolu Agency/Getty Images; cover (bottom-right) Ron Sachs-Pool/Getty Images; p. 6 (background) rarrarorro/iStock/Thinkstock; pp. 6 (top-left), 42 Hulton Archive/Getty Images; p. 6 (top-right) Universal History Archive/Getty Images; pp. 6 (bottom-left), 21, 24, 25, 32, 45, 57 Courtesy of the Library of Congress; p. 6 (bottom-right) Konstik/iStock/Thinkstock; p. 7 (background) Skadr/iStock/Thinkstock; p. 7 (top-left) GERARD MALIE/AFP/Getty Images; p. 7 (top-right) chrisdorney/Shutterstock.com; p. 7 (bottom-left) AFP/Getty Images; p. 7 (bottom-right) SERGEI KARPUKHIN/AFP/Getty Images; p. 9 Keystone/Getty Images; p. 11 © CORBIS/Corbis via Getty Images; p. 13 Olga Popova/Shutterstock.com; p. 15 DeAgostini/Getty Images; p. 18 Interim Archives/Getty Images; p. 22 Bettmann/Contributor/Getty Images; p. 23 Library of Congress, Geography and Map Division; pp. 29, 31, 40 Everett Historical/Shutterstock.com; p. 43 Baturina Yuliya/Shutterstock.com; p. 47 AFP/AFP/Getty Images; pp. 49, 66, 68-69 US National Archives bot/Wikimedia Commons; p. 54 Library of Congress, Prints & Photographs Division, Carl Van Vechten Collection; p. 59 MIGUEL VINAS/AFP/Getty Images; p. 71 VITALY ARMAND/AFP/Getty Images; p. 74 Stiebing/ullstein bild via Getty Images; pp. 76–77 ALEXEY NIKOLSKY/AFP/Getty Images; p. 79 Chip Somodevilla/Getty Images; p. 80 Andrew Harrer-Pool/Getty Images; p. 82 Carl Court/Getty Images; p. 83 ROBYN BECK/AFP/Getty Images; p. 87 Mass Communication Specialist 3rd Class Ford Williams/Defense Video Imagery Distribution System.

About the Author

Gary Wiener is a retired educator, having spent 33 years as an English teacher, department head, assistant principal, and district curriculum leader. He holds a Ph.D. from the University of Rochester and lives in nearby Pittsford, New York. His 23 Greenhaven and Lucent books include *Understanding the Adventures of Huckleberry Finn, Readings on J.K. Rowling, Violence in Suzanne Collins's The Hunger Games,* and *Lacrosse: Science on the Field.* He is the father of two children, Michael and Mollie, and is married to the fabric artist Iris Schifren Wiener.